Building The World's Greatest High School

"For educators and school leaders who long for a positive school culture, the numerous, time-saving, cost-effective methods of identifying and celebrating student success are found in this book."

–**Trevor Greene**, *2013 MetLife/NASSP National High School Principal of the Year*

"As a teacher at the World's Greatest High School, I know that these strategies will work for building strong school cultures and climates. 'Park' started our traditions twenty-two years ago with students, staff and community using these principles and we are still going strong."

–**Debi Weiss**, *Warren E. Shull Outstanding High School Activities Director by California Association of Directors of Activities, Activities Director – Ayala High School*

"I have had the privilege of knowing Richard Parkhouse for over 25 years. His passion for creating positive school cultures is second to none. When he's on your campus, lives change, and students and staff understand the vision while school pride can be seen and felt. His heart and passion are infectious."

–**Janet Roberts**, *CADA President, California Associate of Directors of Activities (2013), Activities Director – Chino Hills High School*

"School culture is the critical ingredient to a great high school. Richard has been in so many schools, his insights and stories inspire and encourage school leaders everywhere."

–**Phil Boyte**, *Learning For Living, School Climate Consultant and Educational Speaker*

"Richard Parkhouse is a thought leader in positively changing campus culture and climate. His insights and observations are 'spot on' and he continues to provide that next step in making our schools the places we all want them to be."

–**Patrick Maurer**, *Speaker and Educator*

"The lessons learned and inspiration gained from Richard Parkhouse lasted beyond my high school years at the World's Greatest High School. High expectations and no excuses push me today as I work in Baltimore City to organize and advocate for ALL children, regardless of race, neighborhood or socioeconomic background, to attend world class schools. If you want to push yourself, your school or your community to excellence, meet the World's Greatest Mentor, Richard Parkhouse."

–**Shannen Coleman Siciliano**,
Former Student

"I have had the opportunity to work with Richard Parkhouse throughout the years and this book reflects his passion for uncovering unique strategies that help support student as well as adult learning. I think this book is a must read for any educator looking for affirmation on the impact of 'outside the box' thinking and leadership as well as examining student motivation from the inside out."

– **Keith M. Bell Sr.**,
Superintendent, Euclid City Schools, Euclid, Ohio

"Richard Parkhouse is a proven performer in helping schools build productive school culture! As a former high school principal, 'Park' helped us instill a caring school climate for all students!"

– **William F. Roberts IV**,
Assistant Superintendent
Hacienda La Puente Unified School District

Visit Park's Website

www.edalchemy.com

Other Works by Dr. Guy E. White

Exiting The Bakesale® Fundraising Training

The First Seven Days: Exciting Step-By-Step Meetings

Get Free Training at Guy's Website

www.exitingthebakesale.com

Building the World's Greatest High School

How to Recognize and Develop the Gifts, Talents, and Skills of All

By Richard Parkhouse & Dr. Guy E. White

Published in collaboration between:

EDalchemy, Inc.

wghs_b1_130620

20687-2 Amar Road, #231

Walnut, CA 91789

Triumphant Heart International, Inc.

12188 Central Ave., #366

Chino, CA 91710

Get free training at www.worldsgreatesthighschool.com

Library of Congress Control Number: 2013932486

Dedication

To those that dare to be better today than yesterday.

Park Acknowledges...

Acknowledging the people who "Changed my Life and Impacted my Future," I have been blessed to be able to have been surrounded by some of the "World's Greatest People." These are the people who have been instrumental in contributing to who I am today and to the World's Greatest Philosophy. "I am who I am today because of these influential teachers, coaches, mentors, family, and colleagues. Thank you to each of you for making me better today than yesterday."

Coach John Scolinos - The Fundamentals of Life: Character, Class, and Compassion. Probably the "Greatest" person I have *ever* met. I thank Coach for stressing that one's success is based on applying basic fundamentals to everything you do. People would say Coach had a drill for everything: even for falling out of bed. He taught us to "surround ourselves with good people, and if you want to know who you are, take a look at who are your friends." He also emphasized, "It is more important to be a Big League Person, than a Big League Player." John had a profound impact on who I am today. The ideas, gifts, talents, skills are released through hard work and focusing on fundamentals in everything you do. He constantly instilled in his players to always compete against the best. By doing this, you will find out who you are. You had to believe in yourself and "Never Give In!" Our team was a Division II team with no scholarship players and we beat some of the best Division I baseball teams, because we were fundamentally sound.

Jim Green - Be Yourself. Jim was my first educational mentor. He taught me to stop trying to be someone I was not. I was trying to be the teacher that I thought I should be instead of focusing on my gifts and how to utilize those gifts to impact others. He provided me a moment that changed my life as an educator.

Glenna Ramsey - The Visionary. The Principal of the World's Greatest High School. She allowed me to be me and instilled a deep belief in what I was doing. She gave me the opportunity to be a part of an incredible team that set out to build the World's Greatest High School back in 1990. Glenna taught us all that the "Most important thing that happens on campus happens in our classrooms." Glenna taught me the importance of trust in people and stressed that "You never tell people 'no' because it is a trust breaker." She never said "no" but you always knew when she didn't think it was a good idea. There were unforgettable times that I told her to "trust me." I never will forget the times she rolled her eyes when I told her what I wanted to do. Glenna had clearly defined Core Values that she lived daily. She allowed the "World's Greatest High School" philosophy to be woven into the daily fabric and culture in everything we did on that campus. She was a true educational leader with great vision for what a school should be for all.

Larry Biddle - The Inspirer. Larry has had incredible influence on creating the power of celebration and instilling the WOW factor into celebrating all stakeholders. Larry has played a key role in where I am today. His influence can be seen in how we celebrate the power of the mind with the same intensity as athletic performers. His mentorship and friendship has played a key role as to where I am today.

Dale Favier - The Activities Guru. Dale instilled the "Why" in student activities. Dale commanded high expectations from everyone around him, and focused on developing a school culture and climate that enabled success. His thoughts and insights were the foundation for building the World's Greatest Activities Program.

Dale had a huge impact on developing a philosophy of inclusion within the school community.

Student Leaders – The Implementers. To the many student leaders who embraced the philosophies and principles: you put them into action and made it happen in a big way. It was truly a pleasure watching you grow and become the "World's Greatest Leaders!"

Dr. Guy White – The Influence. Guy's intellect and, especially, his compassion for student success was the driving force to write this work. It is a privilege and an honor to be a part of Guy's vision and his calling in life.

Our Kids: Alicia, Ricky, and Corrie – The World's Greatest. Each of you embody the spirit of being the "World's Greatest You." Alicia, Ricky, and Corrie each are unique unto themselves. Each possesses their own set of gifts, talents, and skills that make them such special people. Dad is very proud of what you have accomplished and what you will accomplish in your lifetime.

Diane – The Driving Force. I would not be where I am today if not for my incredible bride. She is truly my driving force and biggest supporter. Diane has allowed me to live my passion. I would not be who I am today without her wisdom, insight, compassion, support, love for life, and her belief that all students are gifted and talented. It was her understanding and support behind the scenes that allowed me to pursue my dreams. I am truly grateful for her dedication and guidance. This work is dedicated to Diane.

Guy Acknowledges...

Bringing a book from the heart to the page is a long road - the distance of which is often measured in time: the time to write, the time to sit down and type, or the time to clear the schedule and actually do the work. For me, it took profound mentors to enable me to allow these ideas to germinate, take root, and grow into my teaching practice. It was not until idea became practice that the idea of writing a book emerged. There have been numerous forces that have had an immense impact upon my practice as an educator - few of which came from staff development or common planning time. I had to search for mentors. Fortunately, my mentors found me first.

Richard Parkhouse - Thank you for the World's Greatest that you inspired in me. Thank you for your patience, understanding, and whole-hearted friendship that was one of the most singular forces of inspiration and incitement in my first five years of teaching. Without you, I may have left the teaching field altogether - or, worse, settled for being an "okay" educator.

Larry Biddle - You're purposeful rebellion in all you do is catchy. Your fight against mediocrity inspired me to challenge my administrators, fellow educators, and bored students with uncommon teaching strategies and a teaching philosophy that meets each of my students exactly where they need it as individual learners. Keep the fight going, brother. Thank you.

Laura Divine, Joann Hunt, and Integral Coaching Canada – I had to leave the circle of public education altogether to find the training that you provide – the finest, most meaningful learning experience in my life. My hope is that any educator who wants to build the individual capacities of their students would make their way to your doorstep in Ottawa. Thank you.

Dr. Kristen M. White – My love, my life, my wife: Thank you for your giving heart, your enabling spirit, and all that is within you that convinces me that, together, we can make any dream come true. Thank you for being the kindest, most loving person that I have ever encountered.

The 10/15 – My partners in crime in the University of La Verne Doctoral Program in Organizational Leadership: Thank you for your genuine curiosity and openness. Thank you for allowing me to be part of your lives during our time together in La Verne and for the continued influence that you play in my thinking, my heart, and my teaching.

CADA - The California Association of Directors of Activities: Thank you for the mentorship, guidance, and assistance that you provided me over the past six years. Thank you for pouring into educators and fighting for what is great in education. Thank you for fighting for the soul of the school - the life that happens both inside and outside the classroom.

My Students - Thank you for putting up with my never-ending learning curve - allowing me to experiment with teaching strategies that often made you scratch your head, and, sometimes, made you excited about learning. Thank you for keeping in touch with me and for being forthcoming from your hearts. The trust that you have placed in me over the years is what has enabled me to grow as an educator. In a profession where little makes sense, you make the most sense. Thank you for being real; for bringing that raw energy into the classroom; and for being all that you are in the hallways, in the gym, on the field, and out in the wide-wide-world into which you are stepping. There is so much hope for the future - because the future is you.

Preface

When I first met Park, I was a lost, wide-eyed first-year teacher - having just left my job as a full time restaurant manager - and still feverishly trying to figure out what this whole "teaching thing" was all about. We met at the 2006 convention of the California Association of Directors of Activities (CADA), where I was wandering the halls, overdressed in a button-down shirt and slacks, looking like I had just taken off my apron and walked off the kitchen line to hang out with the wildest bunch of educators I had ever seen. As I have always found at every CADA convention I have ever attended, there is a unique, thriving chord among educators; they understand the value of the intersecting life-changing school experiences happening outside the classroom, intermixing with the heavily regulated in-classroom experiences that are the focus of so many other conventions, conferences, books, and talks. CADA's annual convention has always been different in this respect, because I have always felt like people there "get it" - even when I had no idea what it was I was "getting." It was no mistake that it was in a place like that I first met this guy named "Park."

In a city of prophets, the multitude of voices can sometimes jumble. CADA is like such a city with so many people with such amazing ideas about teaching and learning. Anyone who has had the experience of going to a life-changing conference or convention can attest to the familiar take-away question on the journey home of "what in the world can I take from all that?" Park's words were the answer to that question for me that first year. I attended presentations about how to throw a rally, how to make a good poster, and how to fundraise for those t-shirts I wanted to buy my leadership students. Through them all, I kept hearing group after group of high-energy high school Activities Directors saying that they were going to attend this "Parkhouse" fellow's session later that day. Good people talk about good people. I listened and followed.

The decision to go to Park's session was a life-changing one. For any of you who have had the opportunity to hear him speak, you know two of the major marks of this man's teaching: First, he has an ever-deepening connection to educators and what they do. As an educator himself, he has a great talent toward understanding the state-of-the-art, because he is so actively involved in *listening* and conversing with other educators. Second, he is a mentor who advocates mentorship. I was not just another attendee in his workshop. He introduced himself to everyone in the room, including me, who stayed afterwards and talked. He listened. Many, many conversations arose from that first meeting: he became my mentor that day.

This book is the product of the **mentorship** with which Park has honored me for the past seven years, beginning at that workshop many semesters ago. As I write this preface, I have just come from Park's surprise sixtieth birthday party and feel fully present with the reasons leading to the creation of this work. First, many of us educators can point to an individual, a mentor, who has had a profound impact upon the way that we undertake our art of teaching. What would you do to honor such a person? For me, the answer was simple: Interview him and write about what his philosophy of teaching has meant to me. Second, as educators, we are in need of mentorship in the fundamentals of our art. The evidence of such a need is easily found in our staff meetings, in our hallways, and in the eyes of our students and fellow educators. What would you do as an enduring gesture of love to students and teachers who were in need? My answer to this question: Illustrate the six values that I believe can have a life-altering effect upon any student, any teacher, in any classroom, anywhere. Finally, I hope you will be a mentor too. Regardless of how few or how many years you have been teaching - regardless of how few or many "CE" (continuing education) units you have acquired - regardless of how few or many certifications you have undertaken - you have the ability to be exactly what your students and colleagues need today.

This evening, when Park walked into his daughter's and son-in-law's home to see the dozens of people laughing and loving while firing party poppers at him from every direction, the look on his face reminded me of why we wrote this book. If you could create a school where each student and each teacher felt like they were the guests of honor at a party that *was planned for them in advance*, then you would transform the soul of every student in that place - and, yes, their achievement would follow. In this book, you are our guests of honor. We have been waiting for you.

- Dr. Guy E. White

Table of Contents

Foreword

Shannen Coleman Siciliano

"You are running a million dollar corporation!" was often a line from Mr. Parkhouse (Park). Hearing that would prompt all of my classmates (or what we called our "family members") to remember the importance of the work in front of us. Yes, *our* work: not the work that Parkhouse assigned to us but rather the work we decided to do together. In fact, excellence and high expectations have been a running theme in my life ever since being a part of United Student Body Leadership class of the World's Greatest High School.

Another word for "work" is "passion." During my time in "Leadership," as we liked to call it, our work was more like our passion. Passion coupled with high expectations, led our Leadership Class to stay hours beyond the bell to work on the upcoming pep rally, meet with our class officers to plan the next class activity (from Homecoming floats to Prom planning), or work over the weekends to expand the business relationships that supported our program.

Every year, my Leadership classmates and I arrived at campus at dawn for the first day of school. We made sure that the previous year's faded bulldog paw prints were spray painted on the ground. Posters plastered the school: "Welcome Back! The World's Greatest Students attend the World's Greatest High School! Let's make this a year to remember!" They reminded our other 3,000+ classmates that they were returning to the "Worlds Greatest High School." We lined up the soundtrack so that during the morning and lunchtime, our sound system roared tunes that fit the occasion. Two or so weeks prior to the first day of school, we welcomed back the staff. Each staff member received foiled business cards and a welcome back gift, also to serve as a reminder that they were "The World's Greatest Staff at the World's Greatest High School."

We didn't just talk the talk but we walked the walk! It wasn't enough to simply put up posters throughout the school or hand out new business cards for people to believe the mantra. Every decision made throughout the school was done so in a world-class way. Students owned the culture of the school -- it wasn't force fed to us. The students in the Leadership class felt this ownership heavily; if we wanted to make something happen, we did it. After making sure that every "i" was dotted and "t" was crossed, we presented our plan to Parkhouse using none other than a "Parkhouse Planner." Our Parkhouse Planner was a template to ensure that any idea or event we wanted to pursue was thoughtfully coordinated and carefully planned with our classmates. After all, we were running a million dollar corporation with a lot at stake!

As I left the World's Greatest High School, Parkhouse provided another piece of advice (which I had heard multiple times prior), "Surround yourself with good people!" After graduating, I continued to seek places, organizations and people that exuded excellence and high expectations. I attended the University of Southern California because I felt the strong sense of tradition and excellence throughout the school: from my acceptance packet to football games. I later learned that Park took a few lessons from USC to apply to his teaching. No wonder I felt right at home during my first visit to the campus!

In choosing my career, my first thought was not, "How can I make the most amount of money?" I thought, "What can I do that aligns with my passion? What can I do that will make a difference?" During this moment of questioning, I found Teach for America, a program that places passionate, driven individuals to work in our nation's most underserved schools. As I learned more about Teach for America, the themes of passion, high expectations and excellence came forth once again. I also learned that the organization was extremely competitive and, if accepted, I would be surrounded by some of the best and brightest college graduates in the country.

While teaching in Baltimore City Public Schools, I was placed in a school that would provide development unparalleled to many of the other schools in the district. Teaching was not easy. In fact, it was probably the most challenging yet rewarding experience I've had. What made my experience a positive one was having high expectations for my students and myself everyday. I couldn't allow excuses or too many outside distractions to get in the way of the education of my 2nd graders. I was also surrounded by a wonderful team of colleagues who continued to push and support me during my first couple of years. Over time, I had begun to walk the walk.

Now, after nearly a decade of living in Baltimore, I work for a nonprofit, Child First Authority (CFA). Child First seeks to develop youth by strengthening and reforming schools. CFA provides excellence in school and after-school opportunities for youth while also organizing community leaders to create positive change in their communities.

During my first year at Child First, I was hired to oversee the academic programming and help to organize around issues in education. After working at CFA for 5 months, an article was written in the local paper highlighting the proposed education funding cuts for Baltimore City from the state of Maryland. Four days after the article was written, 30 organizations across the city gathered at the Child First office to determine our plan of action to ensure that $35 million for Baltimore City would not be cut. I felt the passion to stand up and get involved in any way possible. A couple of months later, I was nominated to serve as the first co-chair for the newly created and formalized Baltimore Education Coalition (BEC).

I didn't have years of community organizing experience, but a team of outstanding members surrounded me. Committed teachers and parents, experienced nonprofit and community organizations' staff members, and other more experienced organizers helped to push the coalition forward. From my days in high school, to my time teaching and then working as a teacher coach and lead curriculum developer for Baltimore, I felt prepared to lead.

We established high expectations for one another, our communities and our legislators from the beginning. We worked to ensure that all children in Baltimore receive an excellent education by advocating for effective education reform policies and practices. Since the creation of the BEC, we have prohibited over $100 million dollars in state cuts to Baltimore City Schools. We are currently working to ensure that every Baltimore City school building is renovated or reconstructed in the next 10 years by organizing a commitment of over $2 billion from our state and local legislators.

I've gone from "running a $1 million corporation" or Leadership class to working to ensure that $2.3 billion is committed for Baltimore City's dilapidated school buildings. During this span, excellence, high expectations, and passion have been my guiding forces. I sincerely believe that everyone deserves to walk into a school building with the same belief I held. They should know that they are the "World's Greatest Students, Teachers, Parents" walking into "The World's Greatest Schools."

Note from the Authors

We greatly respect the people with which we serve and the sacredness of our work with students and educators. Accordingly, the names of students, peers, and others in this volume have been changed.

Purpose

The purpose of this book is to inspire and enable you to build the World's Greatest High School – to change lives and impact futures at your school by respecting, celebrating, and cultivating the gifts, talents, and skills of all.

Introduction

"With so many books and speakers out there selling their ideas of what can fix schools, let's step back and start thinking about a new blueprint for a new type of high school that can be created today without laying a single brick."

This book is unlike many in the edu-sphere or those with silly-looking covers sitting on Amazon.com - or like any handed to you by the school administrator who has discovered the "next best thing - the magic bullet for all our problems." This book is built upon a set of principles that will make your reading of this unlike anything you have experienced, heard, or considered before - especially when it comes to schools. It is through living out these principles, or values, that educators like you can create a school we call, "The World's Greatest High School."

What is the World's Greatest High School?

The World's Greatest High School is a place where everyone is becoming the best versions of themselves each day - and these schools *already* exist all over the country. These schools take a radical approach to school improvement. Where some educators tout the mantra of "got a program for that problem?" World's Greatest Educators seek the betterment themselves first, each individual student second, and each individual community member third as their ultimate goal. By becoming masters at a way teaching unique to this school, these educators assist each student in becoming his or her best self, and, accordingly, the fabric of the school and the community surrounding it changes one thread at a time.

The World's Greatest High School is not made up of the top one-percent of students or the best-trained educators. The educators of the World's Greatest High School are like many with whom you interact with each day – each with the key characteristic of wanting to become the best versions of themselves that they possibly can be. They say things like, "I hope I can handle that discipline situation with that student better next time," "I learned this amazing strategy on the internet yesterday and want to try it with my students, and "I want to know what makes each individual student tick." The students of the World's Greatest High School are very much like the students with which you interact on a daily basis too. The key difference is that they have educators, fellow students, and other community members on their side assisting them in developing their own individual growth areas every day. Parents and other supports in this community are also quite similar to those in nearly any school. They care about their students just the same - but they have a whole community assisting them in learning exactly what will make the greatest difference for their individual student. They are the "World's Greatest" not because they are the best in the world like "Worlds Greatest" Olympic Gold Runners, billionaires with bad haircuts, and other one-and-only "top-dogs" that our society idolizes. They are the World's Greatest because they want to be the best ME they can possibly be and help others to do the same. Being "the World's Greatest" could be better stated, "being MY greatest" or, more accurately, the "greatest version of ME." Anyone can become a better version of himself or herself. Any improvement of myself today, is an improvement - in fact, if you become even slightly better at anything than you were yesterday, you are becoming your greatest self. We go a step further: we believe wholly that if you seek to become the World's Greatest Me, others will follow you, and others will follow them. Through seeking to be your best self, your entire school, and everyone in it, can be changed.

Why the World's Greatest High School?

The roles of teachers are greatly changing - it's just that most of the education world has not realized it yet! We are witnessing four trends in education today that are quite pressing on our minds.

First, we see a trend of educators only bringing part of themselves to school each day. We believe that your entire being - everything about you as an educator and all that you bring into your school, is the grandest thing that you can offer to your students, your peers, and your community today. How could more of the best of you impact your students?

Second, we have witnessed an ever-increasing trend, amidst the never-ending change experienced by educators, to just "get by." We staunchly believe that being "okay" is not okay. Mediocrity - doing just enough to get by - is not only undesirable; it is greatly harmful to your students, your peers, and your school community at large as well. Worst yet, it prevents you from getting what you really want. What might you be giving up by settling for "just okay?"

Third, thanks to an ever-growing group of educator change-agents, we have seen amazing turnarounds occur within short amounts of time within the schools that we have visited. We believe that through a single school year of living out the best of yourself, you, your students, your peers, and your entire school community can experience a revolution that will change lives and impact futures of all. How could your school community be impacted by such a shift?

Finally, just as you are reading this book, we see an ever-growing group of educators who wholly reject today's paradigm of "getting by" with unsuccessful students, little improvement, and a school culture filled with other people "okay being okay." We believe that by picking up and reading this book, you are already signaling your opposition to the mediocre tinkering with the school system that we are experiencing today. Already, you may be part of the World's Greatest High School Movement.

While many trends within education seem to be driving teachers to limit their being, impact, and potential, by reading this book, you will see that educators have a chance to be something much more grand than facilitators of proficiency in content standards like those standardized tests make us out to be. In this new era of the "World's Greatest Educator," we educators cultivate the conditions of the human heart that facilitate growth, inspiration, and learning.

Contrary to much of the message out there, which encourages educators to "make it happen," "get 'er done," and set goals, we think that setting goals for future outcomes is only useful if people care about the goals they are setting. Further, we think that the only outcomes worth striving for are those that make our lives better - not more complicated to the detriment of the health, happiness, and expressions of humanity by our students. If you walk onto most high school campuses today, and speak to a "savvy" administrator, they will probably have a form that they give their staff to fill out each year regarding what they want to accomplish with their students. Entire meetings are held for the purpose of explaining the form and giving people time to fill these things out. We own calculators and it does not take much time to multiply the hours spent on this activity by the average pay per hour afforded educators. Millions of dollars each year are spent on goal setting. The sad thing is that most educators will never interact with these goals again after these initial meetings. No follow-up, no reflection - Nothing!

In our view, school "reform" is going to take more than goal setting. School transformation requires personal transformation. The World's Greatest Educator works each day to personally transform into a better version of himself or herself. Rather than being a complicated process of "reforming the school," we will show you a simple way for you, and others around you, to become the World's Greatest Me.

Why Us?

We did not set out wanting to assist educators everywhere to become their "World's Greatest" - much less build the World's Greatest High School. In fact, there was a time when both of us considered leaving the classroom altogether. Beyond wanting to help students and educators, there was nothing in our individual aspirations that would lead us through the front doors of hundreds upon hundreds of schools over thousands of miles. Instead, we had what most of us teachers had - one or more mentors that had a tremendous impact upon who we became - and who we are today. Both of us wanted to step into the role of helping educators, students, and their communities, because both of us have sat where you are sitting - and one of us still teaches full time - and the other spends much of his days visiting the classrooms of others throughout North America.

Both of us could not fully see what it would be like to be an educator in such a place as the World's Greatest High School: even though Park had taught there before! We had a picture in our minds, but we did not have the words. We had incredible experiences as educators, but we did not see how we could communicate them. We were not equipped to tell this story. One morning, however, Park's granddaughters, Kiley and Alyssa, were put on life support and the words became clear. We began to see clearly why now is the time to build the World's Greatest High School.

Why Now?

We stand at a pivotal moment in the story of public education, where we will be soon deciding on one of two very different paths: one ever-focused on scored, bubble-in tests, and the other focused intensely upon the quality of human beings emerging from our schools. The way our lives will be carried out as educators will depend greatly upon which of these two paths we choose. As educators who have stepped foot in nearly one-thousand schools over the past two decades, we know that when educators choose to improve their individual lives, and seek to improve the lives of all that surround them, this is the most powerful shift that can occur within a school.

Further, as we watch what is happening to our school budgets, watch the way that the politicians and policy makers are working with schools, and watch the ways that other "reformers" are dealing with schools today, few are talking about creating the kind of school that delivers the individual success of each student, educator, and community member. Why does so much of the literature on school reform shy away from focusing upon the personal transformation of the educator required to allow change to happen? This book calls for educators to transform themselves to transform their school.

Our hope is that, through this book, we can assist you in building the World's Greatest High School by making the inspiring case for it's existence. Further, by showing you HOW to build it, our hope is that you will be able to find yourself at the end of this school year more fulfilled than you thought previously possible - and in the company of students and fellow educators who are equally bettered. You can build a school where each person there is inspired and able to become the World's Greatest Me each day. Not only have we built such schools ourselves, but also we have seen countless other educators do it without the benefit of this book. All they had was an inspiring idea that was pushing them to "change the way that they were changing their school." They wanted to build the kind of school whose front entrance proclaims, "Through These Gates Walk the World's Greatest Students and Educators."

We honor here what we educators have – because what we have is amazing: We have each other and the ability to become something more. Welcome to your guide to *Building the World's Greatest High School.*

Part I

Laying the Foundations

We believe in compelling visions of the future – and a compelling vision of what you and the rest of the people at your school can be together. In this first part of this book, we'll lay out "the why" of this compelling vision – the big ideas about Building the World's Greatest High School. Then, in the second part of this book, we'll tell you how to build it.

All Kids Have Futures

Chapter 1

"Just like people, all schools have stories. This history is how we went from being a nobody to a somebody. Without this history, we are simply a nobody."

Park was distracted from his students that morning. I was sitting in the front row, stage left, as he was taking 500 leadership students and teachers through his signature routine of leveling-up their energy before a huge day of learning and conversation. Soon, Park would present to these students the same seeds of the World's Greatest Values that he imparted to me, two years before, which changed everything about my way of teaching, seeing, and interacting with my students. Now, these students would hear the values, start living them out, and spread them to their schools and communities throughout the county. It was like watching a doctor injecting much needed medicine into a hurting patient. The kids lit up – but Park was holding back. His heart was elsewhere.

His granddaughters, Kiley and Alyssa were on life support. Late the night before, only hours before our student leadership event, his daughter, pregnant with twins, went into early, distressed labor. When I pulled into the venue that morning to set up registration, a half-dozen of the staff members were already there, surrounding Park – his eyes tired, deeply set in a grey face. Hundreds of students would be here in less than two hours. We collectively decided to support Park in getting the event started, even if he had to leave five minutes in.

This was one of the most stressful mornings in Park's life, and one of the most difficult to be with him as his friend; however, seeing him go through so much pain became a pivotal moment for Park, for me, for us, for our families, our students, and our communities – all because two little twin girls decided to show up early one evening. Hundreds of students gathered at the event that morning, their wide-eyed teachers shuffling them into the auditorium, the clapping and stomping began, the music smashed, and the lights went up. Park began to launch into his talk.

Then he went off script.

Have you ever noticed the entrance of a moment that you know will change your life forever? Have you ever felt your mind and heart go quiet, because they know it's time to listen? Have you ever noticed deafening silence - even when surrounded by the laughing and clapping of hundreds? Have you ever had the experience of being with one of your fellow educators during such a time? Watching Park on that stage that morning was one of those moments for me - as everything got quiet, and he spoke into the microphone.

"When do you pull the plug?" he asked. When Kiley and Alyssa were born, they were no more than five-and-a-half pounds between the two of them. It was scary. Park was talking about tubes, wires, and incubation - life support - not even their skin and lungs were developed. They weren't ready for the world they were placed in. "My granddaughters," he breathed with watery eyes, "are just like some students at your school. They come into a world that they are not yet prepared for and they are considered 'behind' from the second they arrived. Without help, they have no hope. Do you tell these students that they are failures? Do you pull the plug on these students and say 'clearly, you are not ready for this place' or 'you just can't make it here?'"

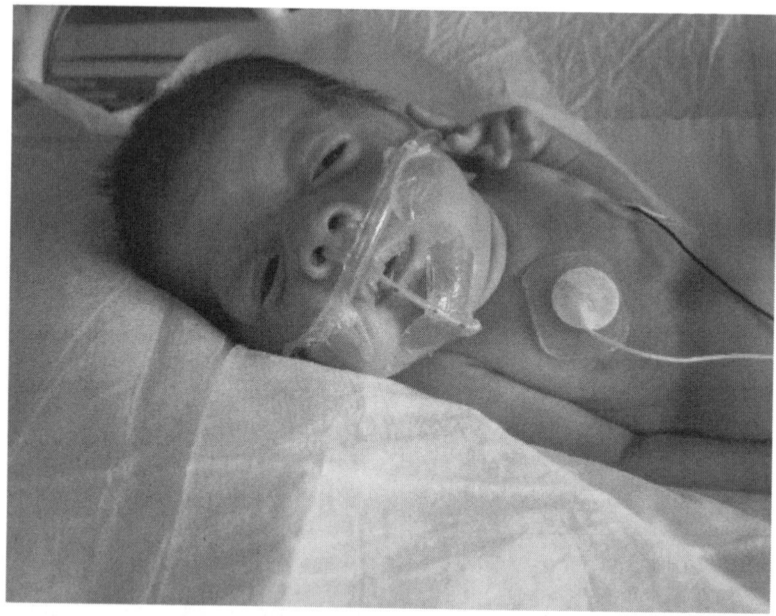

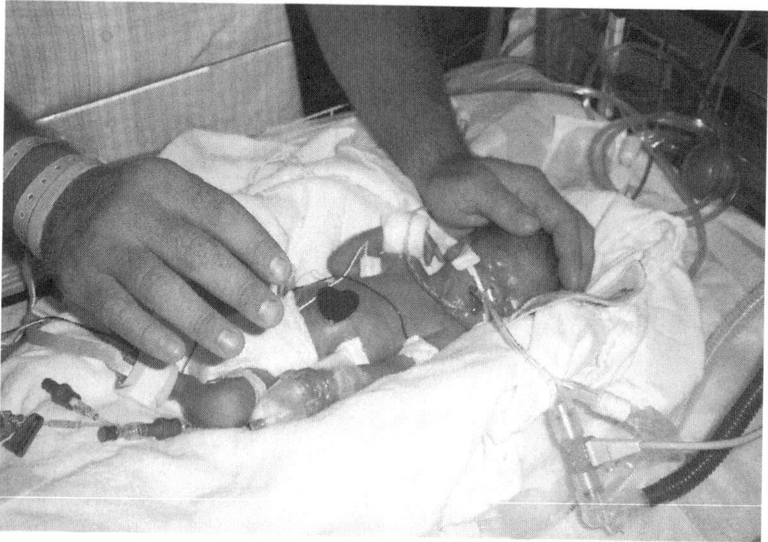

How was I treating the Kileys and Alyssas at my school? I began to think about the students with whom I had worked during my career. I remembered the students with which I had walked down the aisle at graduation, in full cap and gown. I thought of the hours of time in the classroom, sitting in circle, talking about life and literature. Then, I remembered Cody, sitting in the back of my class unengaged, looking at the ceiling - and the day that I confronted him in front of the class and he walked out - and never came back. I remembered Stephanie, and how frustrated I was that she had cheated on her final project just a few weeks before graduation; I was disappointed - but she was devastated when she realized that there was no time to make up the myriad of classes she had failed. I remembered sitting there as she wept helplessly, completely lost. For all the successes with my students, for some students, was I the one that pulled the plug? Did I let them pull the plug on themselves? Could I have done more, earlier?

"My granddaughters are *surrounded,*" Park said, making a full, tight embracing motion with his arms, "by a team of the world's greatest doctors who would never pull the plug. They will use the world's greatest technology and training to help Kiley and Alyssa grow and thrive.

Tomorrow, when you go back to your schools, you give those students the World's Greatest *You* - they need it more than you know. Don't pull the plug on them, because you might be all they have left. Will YOU pull the plug on them, or will you go to their rescue? Will you be nay-sayer who says 'you don't belong,' or will you be the person that says 'thank God you are here - we have been waiting for you?' Will you be exactly what hurting students need today to thrive?" What would it be like to be the best version of myself with my students? How would that impact my teaching?

As these words hit a note of truth in each of the attendees sitting about the room, in me these words resounded a resonating chord of *a monumental shift* within me:

"Some of my students are like Kiley and Alyssa." I thought. "Am I pulling the plug on some of them? Am I just leaving some to fend for themselves? Am I focusing most of my time on the healthy ones, expecting the others to 'get with it?'" These questions sat on me like a great weight - like questions that could not be ignored.

Returning to my classroom in the days after, I remember seeing my students and my interactions with them with striking clarity. I felt immensely uncomfortable in my classroom because my heart, for the first time, was truly recognizing that there were plenty of hurting kids all around me each day - and that little was being done to support them exactly where they needed it most. The idea that Park had put into my head - "Some of your students are like Kiley and Alyssa" - had taken hold in such a way that I was seeing the disconnected eyes of students in the hallways as pain personified. I began seeing low grades as evidence of students feeling lost. I began seeing the "alternative learning center" (ALC) or detention room as the place where students go when the teacher and/or school (at least in part) has failed. I personally began to take more responsibility for my students than I had previously allowed. In all, I started seeing how I was not consistently creating a place in my classroom, much less on my campus, where the conditions for growth and life were offered to each student in the ways that each uniquely needed it most. I was not being the best version of myself that I could be as an educator or human being on campus. This made me *very* frustrated. In all, I felt that I was missing something of key importance in my teaching. Was it possible that I (and so many other educators around me) were missing out on the most fundamental principle of teaching?

In the weeks and months ahead, Kiley and Alyssa found themselves healthy and safely at home with their parents. Park, as many of us that were working with him at the time witnessed, had experienced a very real manifestation of the most fundamental principle of teaching: *We give the kids under our care what they need most – the conditions for growth and life as if "**all kids have futures**."* When our babies are born, we don't lay them on the cold floor, fresh out of the womb, and say "Hey, you down there. Don't you see that this place is all about walking? Get up! Get up, or you will not be able to be a part of all this activity happening around here! Get up, or we'll have to send you somewhere else, where other babies who can't walk are kept." Can you imagine such a thought without something truly painful stirring within your heart? Similarly, is not the most basic aspect of teaching that we give our students what *they* need most? Do we let our students fend for themselves or do we provide them the conditions needed for them to thrive? Park began bringing this message, including photos of his granddaughters to schools throughout the country. He began teaching other educators about the most fundamental principle in teaching: **All kids have futures.** That is, we educators have immense power to provide what our students need to become the best versions of themselves. Meanwhile, back at home, I was feeling the calling that was placed on me to make this overarching value real for my students in the classroom and to tell my peers about what I had learned.

At first, I found myself working with what was in my immediate sphere of control: my teaching and my way of being inside the classroom. I began opening up to my students and being the real me - even by allowing my life experience to become a big part of my teaching through story, metaphor, and honesty about my feelings. I began becoming very protective of my time and energy, and became very choosy about the commitments that I made on campus so I could be more of service to my students and school community. Most of all, I found myself wanting to become the best "me" that I could be in many areas of my life. By the end of the school year, I wanted to tell everyone about what I had learned - even if it made me look crazy. Have you ever been the mad prophet on your campus wanting to share out a great truth that you had discovered? I wanted to tell everyone with whom I met about three major shifts that happened in my teaching when I began believing and acting like all kids have futures:

How Believing 'All Kids Have Futures' Changes Everything

First, when you believe that all kids have futures, your focus shifts to your teaching as a practice - a "practice" of which you have full control. In the Martial Arts, you learn about being "in the Practice" or following "the Practice." This term points to a way of BEING more than a way of doing. You can have all the right moves, but if what's happening on the inside is off balance you'll end up with your face flat on the mat after a kick to the head. Before believing that all kids have futures, my teaching was all about DOING the right things teachers do. When I believe that all kids have futures, my teaching is all about BEING the best teacher that I can be. When class closes and the bell rings, I ask, "Was I what my students needed most of me today? Was I the best me that I could offer today?" *You* become the focus of your teaching, as you seek to become the best teacher in practice you can be.

Second, when you believe that all kids have futures, your students become the focus of the learning in your classroom. How many times have you heard another educator say, "Well, that student simply does not apply herself - she needs to be moved to a different class"? Or, even worse, how many times have you heard, "Not all students will pass; this is how 'success' works. We will always need janitors, groundkeepers, etc."? Beyond the classist ridiculousness of the ideas behind these statements, notice the focus: it's on what students do. Instead, when you believe that all kids futures, the focus is on what student "*can*" do - and the focus is on how *you* can expand each student's capacities to the next level. In this shift, you begin seeing where students are today and ask, "What is the logical next step in this individual student's learning? How can I build a path for him or her as a unique human being to learn what I am attempting to teach?" You focus upon the individual baby-steps of learning in *each* of your students.

Finally, when you believe that all kids have futures, you measure the impact of your teaching based upon evidence of the student becoming a better human being - not just a good test-taker. Much of what we do as educators has, in recent years, been framed in terms of an ever-narrowing set of "results-based" tests, evaluations, and observations. There is definitely a value in these. However, they are simply not the whole story of what is going on for our students, how they are advancing toward the other side of that hill we call "the future," and how our impact upon them is a TWO WAY STREET. Our students don't just benefit themselves - though this is one of the overarching goals of the school - they benefit each other - and they benefit us. No bubbled-answer test, at least that we have seen, gives us the entire picture. So, when you believe that all kids have futures, anything that moves the needle for your students becomes of interest. This may not manifest on an exam right way - instead, you might notice more eye contact, more conversation, more showing up to class on time. A whole world of data at which we don't normally look opens up to us - all because we believe that all kids have futures. What's more, their futures are not often determined by single data points. When you make this shift, you begin to ask, "Did I help this student to be better than the day before?"

We'd like to take a few moments here to acknowledge those of you reading this and saying, "Oh, great. This is one of those get-rid-of-the-test books!" That is not what we are suggesting. Our message is really simple: Some students need more help than others - and some students, more than you know, are on life support at your school. You could be one of the only things that is potentially "good" or life changing about their day. Without you, they might not be here. So who do you want to be? Do you want be the educator who says, "We've given you all the chances possible and now have determined that you have no future here"? Do you want to be the guy that pulls the plug on this student? What gives any person the kind of authority to be judge, jury, and executioner of a student's future? Clearly, there are times when a student crosses the line - and we have laws about those lines. However, what about the student who is failing nearly every class? What about the student who rarely meets the mark of what is considered a "success" at your school? Our clear question: Who do you want to be as a teacher? One that decides when the student has failed so much that there is no further possibility of success? Rather, do you want to be the kind of teacher that meets every student exactly where he or she is and builds upon small successes toward something grand? Our sincere hope is that you want to be that second type of teacher - because those kids in your classroom, they need you to be that "best" version of you: one that believes in the World's Greatest version of them.

Park shares these points like badges of honor that he pins on his shirt and dares people to challenge otherwise. These are the banners that he raises with teachers all over the country every week. This is his day everyday, his life, and his message. For me, the challenge is living up to these values each day - and not feeling discouraged when those with whom I meet don't agree with my view (though I have found many, many whom have become allies). The biggest objection to "all kids have futures" that I have heard is that there is "only so much a single educator can do for his or her students." I see that line in the sand when I see a student failing my course. That failing grade is directly related to the extent to which I could assist that student. Sure, that student did not do the work, and, yes, "that's on them." In my view, though, I hold a lot more of "what's on them," than many other educators are comfortable holding. What's on me? My instruction - everything about it. My classroom - all five senses alive (and, yes, I buy air fresheners out of my own money!). My body and my energy - my sleep and the food I take in impacts my ability to teach. My way of being - from the eye contact, to the calm demeanor, to the jokes I attempt to make, to the stories I tell. It's hard to tell your peers, your fellow teachers, that you feel personally responsible for every "F" in your class. It almost sounds crazy to take some amount of responsibility for the quality of one student's day. For me, the challenge is NOT wanting to be more and more a light to each of these students - even when that pushes my buttons, makes me sleepy, and goes far beyond what ALREADY *every* teacher does beyond his or her job description. My challenge is sometimes feeling lonely in that - feeling like a lonely sage in the city without many people with whom to speak about wanting to be "the best me for my students."

If you are reading this, you are not alone. Many in your staff are ready to join you. Many in your community are ready as well. When I began to see that all students had futures, I was on my own in my classroom, like so many other teachers in secondary education. I did not even know that I already had allies waiting in the wings at my school. Like you, all I had was an idea that seemed both provocative and subversive: that every student has a future they are walking toward - and my job was not to be the gatekeeper to that future, but the person that assisted them in taking the necessary steps forward. You too might be sitting alone right now reading this and thinking, "This sounds great and

I look forward to getting started, but would anyone else join me in this process?" Just when the idea of "all kids have futures" began to reach a tipping point - when I needed to step beyond my classroom to further understand this message and develop myself as an educator - I was fortunate to be surrounded by a cadre of others who were already spreading this idea: Chief of these was Park. I discovered that I was not alone and that there were others championing this cause. Already, Park was building the World's Greatest High School and others were taking part in the fun.

Today, there are those at your school and in the surrounding community that are ready to join you in this quest. You are not alone.

Blueprint Questions:

1. To what degree does everyone at your school have the conditions for growth and life? What's missing?
2. To what degree does your school act in all things as if "all kids have futures?" Where does the school fall short?
3. What is one example of how your school acts like all kids DON'T have futures?

4. What is one example of how your school acts like all kids have futures?
5. How would your classroom(s) be different if you believed that all kids have futures?

Dares:

1. Identify one student that you consider the most challenging in your classes or at your school right now.
2. Think about one thing, even if it were simply saying "hello" to them each day, that would make their life just a little bit better than the day before.
3. Provide that thing to them and pay attention to the results.

Three Types of Schools

Chapter 2

"When I started walking onto campuses throughout the country, I began to see how there were really three types of schools out there."

In Chapter One, you read about how Park and I met - and how I met a group of fellow educators, who would change my teaching and my way of seeing students forever. Park's journey to building the *World's Greatest High School* began years before.

From the start, Park had a mentor that emphasized the fundamentals of teaching. As Park describes, "It started my senior year in high school, where I was playing baseball in my high school. My coach took me out to see the Coach of the college team for which I was hoping to play. Now, when I use the word 'Coach,' I remember the excitement of stepping onto that baseball field at the University for the first time. There was this bald-haired guy, his legs bowlegged, with blue trousers, a white shirt, and a black tie. He was eating a banana. Coach, during that first conversation together, set high expectations from the start, saying, 'It's going to be hard for you to play here: you have to get your hair cut short; we don't allow hair to touch the ears; and you can't have any facial hair. If you can't live with that, you're in the wrong place.' He was trying to see what I was made of from the start."

"Coach was a very unique human being, probably the greatest man I have ever met. He was very simple. He was strong in the fundamentals in everything that he did. He was the introduction of the core values that eventually became the World's Greatest Values that are discussed in this book. He was probably the best 'fundamentals coach' that ever lived. For the first two weeks, we rolled the ball back and forth to each other. We had two players who were about ten feet apart, and we just rolled the ball back and forth. That is how we started learning the fundamentals of proper technique for catching the ball, and then it would move in progression from small group to a little bit larger group. He was teaching us brick by brick. So he was a master teacher and he kept things very simple, but it was all based on the core values and having a strong set of fundamentals. It was in those moments on the field that I learned that it was vastly important to understand the fundamentals of what we are doing as teachers and why we are doing it." This laid the groundwork for Park's first teaching job.

Park's first teaching job taught him that bringing the fundamental pieces of him into the classroom allowed him to teach with greater impact. Park continues, "My first year teaching was terrible. I came into the school half-way through the year, and before my first day teaching, the principal said to the staff, 'We have this new guy coming in, so I need you to send me a list of two or three students that you want to get out of your class so we can fill up this guy's class!' You can imagine the kind of kids that I ended up having that first year. More to the point, though, my teaching was all messed up. I was trying to do the things that 'teachers do' I was trying to teach the things that 'teachers teach.' There was such a disconnect between who I was inside the classroom and who I was outside that I was miserable. One day, one of my fellow teachers, truly a mentor to me, came in and said, 'Parkhouse, I have seen you out in the field coaching baseball, and I have seen you in the classroom teaching - you are two different people! What would it be like to be the same person in both places?' I began to think, 'What would happen if I brought the core part of me into all that I did within the school? What was my best here at this school? I won't be the best me until I challenge myself against my best.'" Park challenged himself to become the best teacher he could be by deciding to bring the best of himself each day.

By the time that Park became the Activities Director of the World's Greatest High School, he began challenging others at his school, including students, parents, staff, and community members to become the greatest version of themselves they could possibly be. In the years that followed, Park began to visit schools throughout the United States to learn the best of each that he could bring back to his own school. It was through these travels that he learned that there are three different types of schools.

Park says, "I have visited three types of high schools:"

No Hope High School

"The first type of high school is No Hope High School. A few years ago, I was in a staff meeting of one of the schools with which I work. I was describing a place where teachers feel that kids don't care, which in-turn translates to the kids feeling that their teachers don't care, creating a place where no one cares. When you speak to the teachers at No Hope High School they say, 'You don't understand our kids; you don't understand where they come from; you don't know their challenges - they can't learn; they can't succeed; they are so busy dealing with today, they can't focus on the future!' As I got to this point in the presentation, one of the teachers raised his hand and asked, 'Are you talking about us? Are you saying that we are No Hope High School?' This was far from my intention - to infer that this school was this kind of high school, but many of these educators in this meeting felt convicted by these words. It is very similar to walking into a gathering of people - you know as soon as you walk in if you are welcome or not, if you will be accepted or not, and feel the emotion of the place. The teachers were sitting in the feeling of No Hope High School and did not like me saying anything that reminded them of that. Walking onto No Hope High School's campus, one can sense the tension and lack of welcome. No Hope High School could have a sign over the school entrance saying, '**You don't understand our challenges.**'"

Mediocre High School

Park discusses this second type of school: "In 1974, in a baseball team meeting at Cal Poly Pomona with my teammates, my coach-mentor John Scolinos ("Coach") told us about how you have to have the ability to 'adjust' if you plan on being successful. As he was talking to us about how we have to learn to make adjustments, all of a sudden, this horsefly started making a big buzzing noise as it bounced off the window of the inside of the classroom. Coach saw this and got wide-eyed. He pointed to this fly and started shouting, 'You see this fly here? You know what he is doing?' We were dumfounded - the fly, of course, was trying to get out. John says, 'The fly is making adjustments. He is bouncing off one part of the window, backs off, and then tries another spot.' He took his pointer finger out and started tapping the glass repeatedly in the same spot. He said, 'If you were this fly you would be hitting the same spot over and over again,' as he tapped his finger wildly on the glass. The key to success is you have to adjust. If you don't make the adjustments, you're going to strike out. Mediocre High is famously where those who work there have no time or desire to implement innovations and strategies. This kind of school says, 'We are fine where we are.' Accordingly, everyone there is 'just fine,' breeding a culture that we are all 'okay.' The top kids will perform well because they are the top kids. The bottom kids will be known in infamy, because they are the worst of the worst at this school. The middle kids will be hopelessly in the middle. Mediocre High could have a sign over the school entrance saying, '**We are okay, being okay**.' If we are not challenging people to make a better today than yesterday, then what is the purpose of school? Are we instilling the belief, 'I can be a better me than yesterday'?"

The World's Greatest High School

Finally, Park describes the third type of school: "The World's Greatest High School focuses on a respect for everyone's gifts, talents, and skills - where I can come every day to become the 'World's Greatest Me.' I am celebrated for my achievements, my accomplishments, and my growth. In this environment, when truly created, all believe that the school is a place where their gifts, talents, and skills are respected, celebrated, and cultivated. The students, teachers, parents, and administrators - everyone may not perform the best, but they believe they can become a better version of themselves each day. For example, Mary was diagnosed at a young age with a very rare disease that the doctors said would probability kill her by age four. It was a miracle that she had lived to her senior year of high school where I met her as a teacher at the World's Greatest High School. Because we were at the World's Greatest High School, we did not focus upon her limitations: instead, we respected, celebrated, and cultivated her gifts talents and skills. Since we were at the World's Greatest High School, we considered ourselves a family of which she was part. The expectations for all were very high. The expectations for Mary were high as well. She thrived as she led a group of scholars out for acknowledgement at an Academic Rally. Every day, as she went from class to class, the World's Greatest High School family warmly greeted her. Later that year, I delivered her cap, gown, and diploma on her death bed. In the hospital room as she lay dying, her expectation was still to graduate. The World's Greatest High School probably has a sign over the school entrance saying, '**Through these halls walk the World's Greatest.**' Mary was inspired and enabled to become the 'World's Greatest She,' even when the chances of success were nearly non-existent. Will you create an environment where all are inspired and enabled to become the World's Greatest Me?"

What Park discovered is that there are values that all the World's Greatest High Schools share. In the next chapter and through the rest of this book, we will be discussing these values and how these values can impact your school in a set of specific, high-impact areas. As you are reading, we encourage you to start asking yourself the blueprint questions that appear at the end of each chapter, as they encourage you to look at that which Coach first asked Park to examine - the fundamentals.

Blueprint Questions:

1. Which of the three types of schools do you think most closely matches yours?
2. What are the qualities of your school that make you say that?
3. How is your school already successful in being like the World's Greatest High School?
4. What is ONE area in which your school needs improvement?

Dares:

1. Share with one other educator your assessment of your school's type.
2. If you are an ASB, Activities, or Leadership director, ask your students...
   a. Which of the types of school do you believe we are?
   b. What value do you bring as a student to the student body?
   c. What do you do for the Kileys and Alyssas in your classes?

The World's Greatest Values

Chapter 3

"So much emphasis is placed on the 'How' of teaching that we forget the 'Why' that really supports the teaching and learning at your school. We need to move from how to why."

In this chapter, Park and I will reveal to you the values of the World's Greatest High School. We will present to you the values that will enable your teaching, your students, your peers, your school, and your community to embark on a journey that will change generations of lives forever. Also, we will lay out the structure of the remainder of this book and give you a concrete guide moving forward so you can make your school the World's Greatest High School.

Before we discuss these values, you might find yourself reading these and saying, "Park, Guy, I can see how I can start living many of these values today in my own classroom - but how do I get others to start living these out as well?" Don't worry! These World's Greatest

Values are not ones you have to shoulder alone - and you don't have to lead an entire campus toward these values all at once. At one school, a teacher found herself extremely dissatisfied with the limited staff development she was receiving. She wanted to live out the World's Greatest Values. This led her to undertake the highest possible level of teaching certification as a way by which to become the best teacher she could be. The next year, others began to follow. Within two years, a whole handful of teachers achieved this major honor. Change can first begin with you, spread to just a handful of people on your campus, and then begin exponentially igniting the hearts of people connected to your campus. Bottom line: it only takes you to get started.

Your journey starts with what we believe - our values - because all of our actions either spring forth from or stand in opposition to our beliefs. The choice is ours each moment of each day to live out our values or to take them up and act like we believe them. As a result, we need to lay out plainly the values of the World's Greatest High School so you can choose to live out these values each day at your school.

Here are *the Values of the World's Greatest High School*:

Value #1: We are what we believe – what we believe unifies us.

At the World's Greatest High School, we know our beliefs greatly influence how our school goes about its work.

What does your school believe? Truly, every group, every organization has a belief system upon which it operates each day. A belief system is a set of ideas that guide the actions of a person or group. In your school, the actions that it takes and the messages it sends (whether it is aware of them or not) is founded upon its beliefs. Everything that your school does is based upon this belief system.

To see belief systems at work at your school, you don't have to look very far. For example, if you look at the way that freshman students are greeted on their orientation day, you'll see the school's beliefs about the value of these students in crystal clear detail. Are they brought into the gym with much fanfare, music moving, barbeque blazing, and students cheering? Or, are they greeted by an administrator in a suit and tie preparing to talk to them about the dress code? Resources, energy, and the way we plan for these students have a lot to do with the beliefs that we hold about students. From the start of the school year, some schools believe that the iron fist of the administration has to be clearly emphasized. Other schools emphasize togetherness and belonging as an integral starting point for students. What makes these schools so different from one another? The belief system each holds.

Similarly, look at the way that your staff interacts with one another. Are they a family who gathers regularly to celebrate each other, mourn losses, and brainstorm solutions? Or, are they feuding clans, separated by buildings, hallways, and corners of the teacher's lounge? Belief systems about "what deserves our time and energy," "how students should be treated," and "how my instruction is impacted by the ideas that others express," have huge effects on the ways that we see our fellow staff members - and how we decide to interact with them as a result. We all have a belief about how much "my teaching" should be influenced by others. We have heard many staff members at the schools we have visited say, "What I do in my classroom is only *my* business." That's a belief - and, chances are, these teachers are not alone on their campus in that belief. Imagine how that impacts their work with students! Think about how such beliefs limited their access to good ideas about teaching. Belief systems matter, because they impact our work with students and our school's way of relating with the community at large.

Consider your graduation and how your beliefs are on display there. At one school at which Park consulted, he took part in the graduation preparation. The first day of the ceremony rehearsals, he arrived in the gym and there was a buzz of excitement - these seniors were going to be graduating at the end of the week! It was time to practice lining up, so the person in charge began passing out cards that denoted the line-position of each student. In very little time, it was exceptionally clear how the line order of students was determined: GPA. If you were the head of the class, you were in the front of the line. If you had a low GPA, you were in the back of the line. Imagine this scene: On graduation day, your son or daughter is walking out onto the field - not by alphabet - but by class rank. Can you imagine feeling the weight of your child being in the back of that line? Can you place yourself in the student's shoes - even if you were an "average" student, seeing an ocean of bodies in front of you? What message does that send? Sure, class rank exists, and, yes, some students will be in back - but what choice brought them there? For this particular school, it sent the clear message of "in what order" we value students at graduation. Everything we do as a part of our school carries a message about our entire value system.

Even the written and electronic communications that we send say much about our beliefs relating to students, parents, the community, and a myriad of other matters related to our school. Every parent in a public school has received a "form letter" with the infamous line, "To the parents/guardians of XYZ," followed by the greeting, "Dear sir or madam." Consider the belief system that such letters communicate: "our messaging to you is completely general and non-specific. We did not take the time to write you a specific letter - but simply merged your name along with a few hundred others. You are one in a few thousand with whom we are communicating today." Could your form letters show your individual care for a family or student? Everything we do communicates something about our beliefs.

At the World's Greatest High School, we want to know two things about our beliefs. First, we want to know our belief system, display it out in the open, and talk about it. We want to know exactly what we believe about the work that we are doing each day. We know that the more we focus upon understanding what we currently believe, and how this impacts the school, the more we are able to augment it for the best impact upon our students, our school, and the community beyond. Second, we want to know how our beliefs are intentionally and unintentionally being communicated each day. This way, we can perfect our messaging to further and further change lives. If the wrong messages are being sent, we want to be aware of that - and we want to send more and more messages that relate directly to our values.

In short, at the World's Greatest High School, we know that we are what we believe. Together, when we take up World's Greatest Values, our teaching and way of being with our students, parents, peers, and community partners is enhanced to an unprecedented level - where lives are truly changed and futures are impacted forever. All that is required to start is to make the decision to take a look at the beliefs that guide your actions and the actions of those around you at your school. Then, with bravery, you can move beyond the beliefs that limit your ability to bless your students - and strongly take up those that are guaranteed to change lives and impact futures.

Value #2: All kids have futures.

At the World's Greatest High School, educators know that every student has a future and that educators have the ability to greatly impact that future.

Do you believe that? In the perfect world, this is an easy question to answer. However, when faced with the daily challenges of working with some students, some educators may balk at this idea altogether. "This student," they might say, "simply does not have what it takes to succeed." Remember Kiley and Alyssa - Park's granddaughters that were born without what it took to survive in the air-breathing world? Many students are just like kids in distress, who need the help of experts to keep their heart moving. At the World's Greatest High School, when we say "All kids have futures," we mean that in all seriousness without any reservation. All kids *do* have futures. The question is: What future will you assist them in creating? Or, will you sentence them to a future of being a drop-out, or worse? At the World's Greatest High School, educators of all kinds, from classroom teacher, to administrator, to field coach, all acknowledge that not only do all kids have futures - we have an immense power and authority to impact that future as well. Literally: We, in part, choose our students' futures.

There are two types of borders that we draw in relationship to students' futures. First, there are the boundaries that law establishes. These include what happens when a student brings a weapon to school, distributes drugs on campus, or attacks another human being. These are lines that are well established at your school. These boundaries represent points of no return established by the law of the land - not by people that are within your school. Once crossed, there is a clear roadmap for the future of these students - including suspension, expulsion, and legal consequences. Second, there are boundaries that *we educators* set for our students. These are not defined by the law. Instead, these are spoken and unspoken policies and beliefs that guide the ways that our students can move within our classroom and school. For example, what are your ways of working with students who are having immense difficulty in your classroom? Do you seek them out? Or do they have to come in during lunch of their own decision? Do you seek out the support of other teachers to help? Or do you believe this responsibility is solely shouldered by the student? Similarly, do you accept make-up work from students? When is the last time that you give them a chance to turn in such assignments? Notice how these boundaries relate directly to our beliefs about success and what "successful students look like." We choose daily who is within the boundary of "potentially successful" or outside in the land of "probable failure." How far are you willing to travel to grab a failing student and assist them in moving toward the land of success?

Now, you may be reading this and saying, "What about the student's decisions to succeed or fail?" We have an immense ability to assist our students, yet there is only so much we can do: right? Our question is, "How much is 'so much?' How much control do we have over our students' futures?" In our experience, the line is not as easy to see as we might feel in the midst of our teaching. This value (*all kids have futures*) focuses upon you, the educator.

How far would you go to assist a student to reach success? When Park's son, Ricky, was in his senior year, he came home one day with his friend, Dee. Walking into the house, Ricky went up to Park while Dee stood silently near the front door and asked, "Dad, can Dee move in with us?" Dee explained to Park that his parents had moved into a fifty-five-plus community, and when the landlord discovered that Dee, also in his Senior Year, was living there, the landlord demanded that Dee had to leave. "You could get some money from the State if I live here," Dee explained, which sent Park's and his wife's red flags up. Park asked, "Money from the State?" Dee explained that he was a foster kid and that he was essentially living on the streets. With the support of Park and his family, and Dee's hard work, he went on to be one of the rare success stories in the foster care system - going to Long Beach State, and becoming a recognized speaker discussing how he met his challenges as a foster youth. With the love and support of one teacher, an entire life can be changed and a whole future impacted. No student is born bearing the curse of a mandated future; we have the ability to shape it and help students reach places not possible without us.

Like Park's granddaughters at their birth, many of your students are on life support. You have the ability to choose whether or not to pull the plug. Do you want to be the person who finally says, "Sorry, you simply are not made for this place. It's time for you to go"? Or, would you rather be the skilled, expert physician who gets under the skin, examines what needs to be done, and works with the student to make *some* progress toward "health?" At the World's Greatest High School, educators choose to be skilled at being students' greatest believers - even when the student has already given up. As experts at their art, these World's Greatest Educators can see potential where few can. Each day, you have the ability to see in your students more than they see. Will you help them see the future that they don't see? Will you defend that future from others at your school that are ready to extinguish that future? You have the ability to be your students' greatest ally, simply by believing that they are going somewhere and helping them take even just ONE step toward it.

Value #3: No one gets anywhere without a teacher.

At the World's Greatest High School, educators recognize that no one gets anywhere without a teacher and that the impact of teachers is exponential.

Do you remember the names of your elementary school teachers? Can you think of one teacher in your life that made a major difference for you and your life? No one - absolutely no one on the planet, gets anywhere without a teacher. Think about that: Everyone on the planet has depended upon a teacher, master, guru, or caretaker in his or her life, at some time, to become a better human being. These teachers take many forms and don't always carry the title of "teacher," but, nonetheless, have made it possible for those they serve to be "better." For those of us who have taken on the role as teacher in a classroom, there is something truly sacred about that - as our entire position is about that calling to assist others in becoming better human beings. At the most basic level, the World's Greatest High School acknowledges that teachers contribute to each student's ability to be a success. However, at an even deeper level, the World's Greatest High School recognizes that teachers are often the deciding factor in whether or not a student grows.

Teachers can decide if they solely want to serve the "Austins" of their class - or if they will serve all students. Austin is Park's grandson that was born after his preemie granddaughters Kiley and Alyssa. Unlike his granddaughters, Austin was a big baby (ten pounds, elven ounces). From the moment he arrived in the air-breathing world, he was advanced, skipping newborn clothes entirely and wearing three-month-old clothes and diapers. In everything he did he was ahead of the curve. He's like your advanced kids. So, in your class, you can decide every moment if you will serve the Kileys and Alyssas (the students who need much extra support), the Austins (the advanced students), the students in the middle, or all of the above.

One teacher describes how she served the individual needs of her students: "When I came to my school and met my senior students for the first time, our English department was divided into three categories. At the top, we had Advanced Placement students who were vying for four-year college acceptance. In the middle, we had "college prep" English for students who were bound for two-year junior colleges. And then we had 'Regular English' (at least that's what many of our staff called it). I came into my senior, Regular English classroom mid-year and these students had been with a string of long-term subs for the first half of the school year. I'll never forget the first day saying, 'Take out any of your written work for the past week or two,' and them blankly looking at me, one of them saying, 'Ms. Sam, we mostly have been doing crafts in here.' Looking at the collection of hand-crafted, cardboard shields on the wall, clearly from a Beowulf unit, we began a discussion where I learned that many of my students, when completely honest, had not opened their textbook outside the classroom the entire year. Fast-forward to the end of the school year, when they were openly taking notes from the text, discussing it and analysing it in cooperative groups, and making huge cognitive leaps that related to their own lives - and sharing these openly in the classroom. I knew very solidly that I, along with the rest of our teaching team that year, had an immense impact upon these students." Ms. Sam chose to serve the Kileys, Alyssas, Austins, and all other students in her class. She played to their strengths.

Your students would not be the same without you! Take a moment to think about a student upon whom you feel you have had a profound impact. How has his or her life been enhanced by your presence within it? How would his or her life be less without you being involved? Can you answer these questions? We have worked with thousands of students over the course of our careers and we can picture hundreds, of faces of students that have been impacted by our instruction. In our opinion, teachers often don't "own" that role very well at their school. Park will tell you quite easily, "I change lives and impact futures." Are you willing to make such a bold statement? At the World's Greatest High School, educators of all kinds own the role of someone who "changes lives and impacts futures." Your reach to "do good" as an educator probably has more depth than you know. Let's take a moment to look at that depth.

My leadership class, like many leadership classes (sometimes called ASB or USB or student government classes) became what some educators might call a "dumping ground" for our students who needed massive amounts of support. In the years that I taught that leadership class, I saw some of my most heart-broken students find massive healing through the world that we created together within that classroom. One student, Celeste (not her real name), lost her father when she was less than ten years old. At one time, she was a gregarious young girl who would dare people to prove her wrong, but by the time that she arrived in our leadership program in 9th grade, she was exceedingly withdrawn. Celeste would walk into class, keep her eyes down, and walk to the back of the classroom and sit down. When we would break into groups, she would just sit there, waiting for someone to grab her. I remember one day after attempting to get her engaged with a group, another student walked up to her and said, "Celeste, I hear you are really good at ripping the poster paper. We always screw that up. Can you help?" Over time, multiple students began befriending her and inviting her to take part in their worlds. By the end of Celeste's four years in my program, she was leading it. The lesson I learned most clearly from Celeste is that **your students are proxies of you**: They become your hands, eyes, ears, and living expressions of your way of being in the classroom. When you create a teaching environment that instils your heart for students inside of them, students begin taking up the mantle of caring and developing others - often in ways that we could not, because of their unique roles as peers.

At the World's Greatest High School, educators recognize that no one gets anywhere without a teacher. They also recognize that the impact they make is exponential - not sequential. "Exponential impact" means that the good that you do is not simply added up one student at a time. Instead, your impact is *multiplied* as you affect one student, who interacts with dozens of other people, and hundreds from there. Your influence upon a single student can impact a generation of people in no time flat. Educators recognize that they have influence on students and their futures - but, at the World's Greatest High School, educators own this ability to change the lives of so many people and augment their instruction to have maximum yield of impact.

Overall, educators who embody the World's Greatest Value of **no one gets anywhere without a teacher** take three steps to create maximum impact for their students. First, they recognize where students sit today using heart, as well as eyes. They see where students are in terms of "seeing" grades, test scores, behavior, etc. However, they also "feel" the student's heart coming through their interactions - or lack thereof. Second, these educators help students create a vision of a grand, compelling future. These educators recognize that many students are limited to what they have seen - and some students have seen very little in their lifetimes. So, these educators show them possibilities that these students have either never considered or have long written-off as impossible. These educators place these students in the midst of that possibility and encourage the students to play therein. These can take the form of challenging assignments, imaginative activities, or compelling conversation. Finally, as each student engages with his or her own heart and mind, as well as those of others, the instructor takes the final step of creating life-changing impact upon them: The instructor shows students that they are *already* gifted and talented.

Value #4: All students are gifted and talented.

At the World's Greatest High School, educators seek out and celebrate the gifts, talents, and skills that each person brings into the school.

On the most fundamental level, all students have gifts, talents, and skills. The question is: Will you be the skilled, heart-connecting educator who recognizes these and uses them for the good of your students? If your student is homeless and sleeping in an orchard, they are probably not going to be getting recognized for their talents by their parents. Park recalls visiting a school in Washington and watching the practice drills of the JROTC rifle team. One of these students moved with such precision, skill, and dedication to her craft. After Park remarked to the teacher in charge about being so impressed, the teacher nodded and said, "Yeah, she's homeless." Recounting the story today, Park says, "When I heard that, my heart dropped. That is simply not in my field of vision as I've been so blessed, like so many teachers who are in the school. I can only imagine what it is like to live in a car or in a field at night. But this young woman was so positive about what was happening for her and her life – and it was a teacher who was there promoting her and focusing her on connecting with the gifts, talents, and skills that she was perfecting on campus. Why is it that some students make it and some don't?" What makes the difference for those students is that someone connects with them, believes in them, and works with them to develop those students' gifts, talents, and skills. This allows them to make a future. You may know a student who comes to your school only for the purpose of developing themselves in band, dance, poetry, art, or, even, beat-boxing – and they take part in the rest of the learning program at the school, simply to have access to a place that develops them in that one area of interest.

Many educators have an exceedingly limited vision of what gifts, talents, and skills they recognize in their students. How many times do we see classrooms operating in the modality of "sit down, shut up, and get to work"? Park describes, "I remember walking into Diane's, my wife's, classroom and seeing students with crosses tattooed in the center of their foreheads – but they were performing well! Diane could tell me how each of her students had an individual skill that was unique for that student. When she would speak publicly in front of a student with calm respect about that student's unique skills, the student would beam with pride. As a result, his or her other skills would improve." When we provide students the ability to be "great" at something - and truly develop them in that skill, students' other skills are enhanced as a result. Our focus as educators needs to expand to see a more full vision of whom each of our students are and what value they bring to our school.

At the World's Greatest High School, educators seek out and celebrate the gifts, talents, and skills that each student brings into the school. Did you learn about "prior knowledge" in your teacher education program? Have you heard that term discussed in staff development events? Many educators have taken this to be a very limited set of skills - only related to the task at hand in the classroom. When an educator is teaching about writing an essay, he or she may look only for the prior knowledge regarding paragraph structure, writing a hook, or using the right grammar. The educator can be so focused upon the parts of the engine, that they forget about the frame and wheels that allows the vehicle to move forward - the educator is so focused upon what the student knows about writing an essay, he or she forgets about the capacities that make the student the kind of person that would or could write such a thing in the first place. In the case of many of my own students, they come to school because of the social stratosphere and the gifts, talents, and skills they have to connect with other human beings. Some students come to school because this is the place where they can forward their gifts, talents, and skills in the athletic arena. Some students come to school because they have immense musical ability, and this is the one place where they can exercise that ability. What happens when I ignore this in my classroom and don't recognize, draw out, and celebrate these gifts, talents, and skills? Students only get to bring "part of themselves" to class. Some students may decide not to come altogether.

You may be the only human being in your students' lives that celebrates them. When I first began working with my leadership students, there were four freshman girls that were completely failing out of their content classes. By the sixth week of school, it was clear that these students were going to have to repeat much of their school year if this trend continued. One day, I was walking around campus after school and found these four girls with a battery operated music player and speakers practicing dancing in one of the back hallways. "Why are you practicing back here?" I asked. They replied, "Because we're trying to get perfect before we show this to anyone." Here are these freshman girls - who, for all intensive purposes are doing very little in their classes each day, dedicating two hours, five days per week to perfecting their dance moves. Just as we finished talking, their battery began to die and the dancing was over. "I'll make you a deal," I said. "You can run an extension cord from my room and practice out in the courtyard there, if you'll go through your homework for fifteen minutes with me each day." These daily practices became a ritual, where they would come to get the extension cord and we could talk about their classwork. So much work was put into those students by a whole team of educators - and by me connecting with them over their greatest passion - dancing. I could have written off their dancing as a "distraction" from their homework. Instead, we turned it into what often became a one-hour of dancing, one-hour of doing work and having conference time. You have a similar ability to connect with what students do best. Will you utilize the gifts, talents, and skills of your students to have them connect them to the work inside your school?

Therefore, at the World's Greatest High School, educators recognize that **all students are gifted and talented**. They know that it is often from these gifts, talents, and skills, that each student's future springs. Like skilled trainers, these educators take specific steps to utilize students' gifts, talents, and skills for the furthering of the developmental goals that the school holds for each student. First, these World's Greatest Educators provide opportunities for students to demonstrate their capacities from the first moment they step on campus. Second, these educators publically and privately celebrate these gifts, talents, and skills and put them on display as part of the fabric of "who we are" as a school community. They say, "Look at who we are! This talented student is one of us and represents another amazing thing about our community." Finally, these educators take the masterful step of carefully crafting a learning environment and learning experiences that allow students to develop their gifts, talents, and skills.

Value #5: Everyday is an opportunity to become the World's Greatest Me.

At the World's Greatest High School, each person on campus seeks to become a better version of "me" than the day before – and its members work purposefully to develop each person's gifts, talents, and skills.

So much of the way that we "measure" what students and educators do is based upon management-by-exception – the time that you get the most attention is when something is going wrong. Unless one is of the top ten-percent of the student body or a nationally recognized educator, the *most* attention is given to those who are not performing well. Consider the psychology of this – only receiving attention when you are underperforming. What does that do to the members of your school community over time? At the World's Greatest High School, since gifts, talents, and skills are recognized systematically and celebrated openly, all have the ability to be developed in that individual skill – and other skills alongside. For students, they are recognized for being "great" at something – even if that is simply having the dedication to walk two miles to school each day. Accordingly, the student recognizes the skills in which they are excellent, and along with educators, can utilize that skill to be the springboard for their future development. For educators, they are recognized for being "great" at some aspect of their teaching – whether it is the systematic way in which they utilize a textbook or the strategies they use in their instruction. Similarly, educators can then utilize their existing greatness as a foundation toward developing in other areas. All it takes is recognizing where one was yesterday, and how they are growing today.

Have you ever heard a principal shouting, "shoot for 800!" or any other test score, for that matter, at a student or staff event? This fails to recognize three things. First, people need to know where they are currently standing to be able to understand where they need to develop. The score of "800" means as little to the student as any other number that the principal could shout – especially when the student does not know their previous score. If each student was handed a sheet as they walked into that event stating plainly what their scores currently are, they would better understand where they stand today in those associated skills. This alone, however, does little to assist in this situation. Second, people need to see a compelling, heart-connected reason to reach for a different future. What happens if these students do nothing to improve their scores? Is there a compelling reason for change to occur? No, the principal shaving their head is not enough – there truly has to be a compelling reason that individually appeals to each student - and rarely do schools serve up that kind of vision for the uniqueness of each pupil. If students could recognize on a deeply personal level how doing better in the Language Arts would impact their future self, then they would have much more of a reason to do something about it. Still, however, this is not enough alone. The final piece is the most difficult to deliver. People need to understand how to utilize their current capacities to expand their personal areas of development. Athletes need to understand how to use their skills in endurance and determination in developing their ability to factor equations. Musicians need to understand how they can use their ear for detail in writing an essay response. Social students need to understand how to translate their capacity for discussion into academic language inside the classroom. In short, at the World's Greatest High School, every day is an opportunity to become the World's Greatest Me, because, there, people show me where I stand, assist me in envisioning a future I am hungry for, and show me how I can use my current gifts, talents, and skills to reach that future. Will you deliver that to your students?

At the World's Greatest High School, educators take specific steps to assist students, fellow educators, and community members in becoming the World's Greatest Me each day. First, educators assist each person in discovering the unique gifts, talents, and skills that he or she holds and which specific skills need development. Also, educators celebrate these gifts, talents, and skills as they discover them. Second, educators assist each person in crafting a compelling future that suits that unique individual. Finally, educators assist each person in developing their existing capacities of greatness alongside those skills that are in need of development, simultaneously.

So, reach out and discover the gifts, talents, and skills that you, your students, and your fellow staff members hold. Celebrate these. Explore potential futures with one another that are exciting and represent each person's unique desires for themselves, their families, their peers, and their communities. Build learning and developmental experiences where the capacities currently held can be used to shape skills needing development.

Value #6: Everything we do, we do with PRIDE.

At the World's Greatest High School, the school's one-of-a-kind culture of "Greatness" is clear in everything it does.

Take a field trip to your front office at your school. Walk right in and locate the dusty plaque or hanging frame that contains the school or school district's mission statement. Chances, are, if your school is like so many others, you'll see a paragraph-long sentence, created by God-knows-who by the hard working educators of *whenever*. Every school touts that it has a "mission," but how many are living out that mission – and how many of those missions are truly reflective of the values that each person within the school (including the community members that support it) holds and lives out each day? Our guess is that paragraph in your front office is simply "art on the wall" – that is, it has little relevance to what each person does at that school each day. If you disagree with this, ask yourself: can you recite the mission statement of your school by heart? If not, does that mean you are not living up to that vision? All that means is that a mission statement is only as important as its relevancy to the day-to-day lives of each person within the walls. At the World's Greatest High School, you don't have to guess what the school is all about, because it is clear in everything it does. It's not about a mission statement: it's about living a "way of life" on campus and being able to observe that way of life plainly in every expression of your school.

One of the World's Greatest High Schools that Park helped open in Southern California took this "way of life" thing to the level that we are discussing here. Before the school even opened, members of the future student body, parents, faculty, and people from all around the community were gathered into a room and began drawing out visions of the purpose of the school. They literally sat together and drew out posters of what the purpose of the school was and how the day-to-day life of the average student and how the school would support them toward their future. When the students were greeted on the first day of their freshman year, on the first day of life on this campus, they were brought into a graduation-style celebration, where there was this immediate connection to the vision of what students were working four years to accomplish. Teachers and student leaders together celebrated the students as they entered their freshman year. Throughout those first four years, students were constantly reminded of the vision that was created in those opening breaths of the first day of that school. Further, the staff, parents, and students were also deeply connected to the vision they had created even before the school had opened its doors. They did not create a mission statement – they were on a mission.

Actions speak louder than words. The World's Greatest High School builds a system of values and clearly displays that way of life to all. How does your school express it's unique culture consistently to the world at large and to its members within? How does what happens inside the classroom reflect this way of life? In-between classes? Outside class and on the field? Notice, it's not about the mission statement, or the goals of the school, or what is being said inside a single staff meeting – it's all about what your school says in everything that it does. So many schools say that they "develop each student," yet fail to develop whole groups of students regularly. So many schools say they "expect learning results," yet don't have a concrete system in place to actually assist students who are not meeting those expectations. So, at the World's Greatest High School, we focus upon the messages that we are sending in all that we do - not just in the messages that we intend to send.

Summary

In this chapter, we presented the six World's Greatest Values to you. These values are not what we hang up on a wall and say that we "do them" - they are the fabric of what we hold as true as The World's Greatest High School and our actions show it.

Value #1: We are what we believe - what we believe unifies us.

Value #2: All students have futures.

Value #3: No one gets anywhere without a teacher.

Value #4: All students are gifted and talented.

Value #5: Everyday is an opportunity to become the World's Greatest Me.

Value #6: Everything we do, we do with PRIDE.

In short, these values are the foundation upon which your school can create its unique expression of its own greatness in the world. It does not stop with these values - these are simply the foundation upon which you will Build the World's Greatest High School.

Blueprint Questions:

1. What are one or two values that you already believe? How does that show in your teaching or work at your school?
2. What World's Greatest Values above were "questionable" or ones about which you disagreed? Why?
3. Is there a value that you believe your entire school has already taken up and lives it out each day?

Dares:

1. Choose one of the values above that seems particularly challenging to you.
2. Do one thing, regardless how small, in your classroom or on your campus in the next twenty-four hours that appeals to this value in some way.

The World's Greatest Values

Value #1
We are what we believe – what we believe unifies us.

Value #2
All students have futures.

Value #3
No one gets anywhere without a teacher.

Value #4
All students are gifted and talented.

Value #5
Everyday is an opportunity to become the World's Greatest Me.

Value #6
Everything we do, we do with PRIDE.

www.worldsgreatesthighschool.com

Part II

Building It

Now, the foundations are set and you are ready to learn how to *Build the World's Greatest High School* value-by-value. In this section, we'll take you through seven areas in which you can create the greatest impact today. Then we'll present how you can take this transformation to a level that defies mediocrity and embodies imagination.

World's Greatest Expectations

Chapter 4

"Create a school where success is seen as the norm. If you are told enough that there is no hope, then there will be no hope. If you tell others enough that they can be their greatest, they start believing it and start acting like it."

The foundations are now set for you to begin Building the World's Greatest High School. You see how understanding and holding the World's Greatest Values is the first step along your journey - but it is only the first step. The key to building this school is about living out those values - rather than simply believing them. How do you actually live out the values in a way that creates change in your school? How do you ensure that these World's Greatest Values don't become like other meaningless mission and vision statements at your school? How do you employ these values to make amazing change for the people connected to your school? The rest of this book is dedicated to answering those questions.

We have hand-selected seven areas within your school that you can address immediately to achieve immense impact. There are really unlimited areas upon which we could focus. However, if we were to list all the possible areas of influence in which you could employ the World's Greatest Values, this book would be a massive tome – and an ineffective way of training you to build this school. The seven areas of focus upon which we will be focusing are the most critical and vital ones for you to address. Similar to constructing a house, there is no use of hanging pictures on the walls until the walls themselves have been constructed. Similarly, there is no use in talking about how to employ the values of the World's Greatest High School in the areas of least influence until we have covered those areas that will have the greatest impact for the school. So where do we apply our focus *first*?

As a whole school, the most fundamental area within which we can apply the World's Greatest Values is in the expectations that we hold for our students. "Expectations" is a word that we throw around in education a lot, right? From the "classroom expectations" that many teachers have parents sign each semester, to the expected school-wide learning results we may have posted in our classrooms, to the word being uttered in student-administrator meetings, this word has a lot of baggage in the edu-sphere. *Expectations are simply the anticipated futures that we hold for ourselves, our peers, and our students.* They have immense power because they shape the way we act toward others. That's why we want to start by talking about how you can employ the World's Greatest Values in regards to your expectations *first*, before anything else - because expectations are often where we build our way of seeing the world today, and our way of anticipating the future. What happens when our expectations are out-of-sorts with the hope that we have for our students? What if our expectations are incompatible with the goals that we have for our students? What do we do then? Value-by-value, this chapter will provide clarity about how to strategically infuse your "expectations" with the World's Greatest Values.

Value #1: We are what we believe - what we believe unifies us.

At the World's Greatest High School, we know that our beliefs greatly influence our expectations of what success looks like and for whom it is possible.

The people at your school form a unique culture based upon the beliefs they have. When educators believe in the World's Greatest Values, their expectations regarding students, parents, and the community greatly change. Does your school believe that all students within it can learn? Does your school believe that all students can learn at high levels? Do you believe that each student has an innate desire to become a better person on some level? Do you believe that all parents want what is best for their students? The answers to these kinds of questions say a lot about what expectations your school holds regarding the people it serves.

Our beliefs have a significant impact on what we do and say. Park often tells a story about one of his family members who simply does not have the filters that you and I have in terms of what should be said versus what should not be said. She expects that anything happening is worth discussing – even if it is a sensitive topic. Once, at a funeral, she spoke rather loudly in the back of the room during a quiet moment of the service, "Wow, I wonder if he [the man in the casket] has any shoes on!" Where the room was shocked by what she was saying, she believed she was being truthful and honest. Similarly, if we believe that certain ways of behaving on campus are permissible, we act accordingly. When we believe that our students have immense potential to do well, our expectation of them doing well is enhanced. We act as we believe.

On the most basic level, at the World's Greatest High School, educators are very concerned about what expectations they hold about those with whom they work and those whom they serve. They take steps to understand and shape their expectations about success. First, each asks himself or herself, "What do I expect of my students, peers, and community?" Second, each asks, "How do these expectations show up in my teaching and way of being with my peers, parents, students, and community? Do these expectations shut down or open up my ability to serve them best?" Third, that as a whole, the school makes an intentional effort to get these expectations stated in a safe, public arena, such that these can be examined and better understood. Finally, the school, with key representatives from each group within it, meets together to spell out truly what makes up the expectations embedded within the school's culture.

Value #2: All students have futures.

At the World's Greatest High School, educators expect that every student has a future and that the school has the ability to greatly impact that future.

There are many educators who simply don't believe that all students can succeed. We observed a teacher training a number of weeks ago where one teacher remarked, looking at a group of teachers from another school, "Well, at least at our school and our parents care about their students succeeding and, at least, our students have the ability to succeed." The judgment that educators have about students' futures is the *second* most powerful force in the school - because it carries an authority that greatly influences the *single most* powerful force in the school - each student's belief in his or her own ability to succeed. When an educator works with students believing that they have no future and little chance of success, the students know it and start acting like it. At the World's Greatest High School, educators know that they hold this kind of power and actually take steps to ensure that success is seen as the norm at their school.

When Park was building the World's Greatest High School, the showcasing of this belief that all students have futures did not start at the freshman orientation - it started at the 8th grade orientation across town. Before the high school took on its next wave of students, Park, a core group of teachers, and leadership students visited their "feeder" junior high to set the tone for the upcoming year before these eight grade students would make it into their school. The bar was set very high from the start as leadership students discussed how being at their high school enabled them to become the best versions of themselves and allowed them to show off what they did best. The junior high students got the feeling from the start that going to the World's Greatest High School was a great gift, because success was ALREADY the norm there. Students love to be part of something successful, exciting, and pre-planned. From the start, they got the feeling that they could expect great things for their own futures because the school expected great things from the students there already. To what degree does your school communicate through action its expectation that all kids have futures?

At the World's Greatest High School, the educators, students, parents, and community members band together to teach the school's expectation that all kids have futures. In every interaction, event, poster, Individual Education Plan (IEP), expected school-wide learning result, etc., there is a way in which you can teach the high expectations that your school holds for the heroes that walk through its hallways. Your school can choose to hold the baggage of "There is no hope here" or "We're okay just being 'okay.'" Alternatively, your school can choose to hold with pride the expectation that "All kids that walk through these halls are going somewhere, and we expect great things from them." Which choice will you and your school make? How will you show that?

Value #3: No one gets anywhere without a teacher.

At the World's Greatest High School, educators recognize that no one gets anywhere without a teacher and that the impact of teachers is directly related to the expectations they hold for their students.

In the previous chapter, we mentioned a student who was part of the JROTC drill team who was amazingly talented and was finding much success at her school. Park was surprised that this homeless student could be doing so well, given the challenges that she was facing being homeless. One of the things that made the most difference for this student was the fact that she had a relationship with an educator who not only expected great things "*for*" her, but also great things "*of* " (or from) her. When educators hold high expectations for their students, a transformation toward those expectations is much more likely than if the teacher believes less in that student. How can a student excel when they are told directly and indirectly that they are not capable or likely of doing so? Educators hold such great power in terms of the expectations they hold. At the World's Greatest High School, we acknowledge that power and use it.

At one high school, there was a teacher interested in helping freshman students at her school. For years, she had watched each successive class of freshman come in a little less prepared than the class before. There were many reasons for this, but she knew that what she could control most started from the moment they walked onto campus for the first time. If she could create a "powerful start," showing off the high expectations that the school held for each freshman, then great things could happen for them as the year progressed. The expectation that the school held at the time for freshman - as spoken by one nay-sayer there was - "there is no way you can get 300 freshmen to show up for a freshman orientation and participate in anything more than a dress-code talk for fifteen or twenty minutes." Up until that time, freshman orientation was simply a time to hear about dress code and discipline from a few administrators, and then get your ID picture taken. In defiance, this teacher put together the most exciting freshman orientation ever seen by the school - complete with student mentors, small groups, and students talking with students about success. She set a new bar for freshmen and showcased the high expectations the school had for these students. As a result, the freshmen had a whole new way of behaving on campus - simply because high expectations were communicated in an exciting way. This all occurred because one teacher decided to make this change happen on campus.

At the World's Greatest High School, since the relationship between students and teachers is so instrumental in high expectations being communicated, the school takes steps to place students in multiple opportunities to hear these expectations voiced and see these expectations alive in the day-to-day life of the campus. In short, students are intentionally paired with teachers who will communicate these expectations to them in constructive ways, from the classroom, through the hallways, and onto the sports field.

Value #4: All students are gifted and talented.

At the World's Greatest High School, educators expect all students to bring gifts, talents, and skills into the school.

One of the worst things about going to No Hope High School is that there is the belief on campus that "most students don't bring any skills into the school." The focus here is greatly upon the deficit of all students - and the students feel that and often fulfill this expectation by bringing as little to the table as possible. Who, after all, wants to bring anything to the party when they are not welcome there? Similarly, at Mediocre High School, there is a pervasive feeling of "we're all okay and we don't have to be 'great,'" to such a degree that any skill is seen as just another reason we're "doing okay." Here, students don't get celebrated for being talented; they get a resounding yawn. At the World's Greatest High School, great things are expected from all students and all students are celebrated for what they bring into the school. Everyone has the chance to feel like they are part of the Royal Family because everyone is celebrated for something they bring. *Everyone* brings something of value to the school.

To illustrate the necessity of making everyone feel like they have value in the school, Park uses his trademark playing-card activity at staff in-services he leads. In a room of educators, he passes out the contents of a deck of cards, one card to each person without him or her seeing what card he or she has been dealt. The cards are equally divided into four card types: Aces, face cards, number cards, and jokers. Once everyone receives their card, they are instructed to place the card on their foreheads without knowing what group their cards represent. Each participant responds to the specific card on the other peoples' foreheads: Aces are told "they are fabulous;" face cards are told "I saw you at the game, getting an A on the test, etc."; number cards are only looked upon with no conversation; and when one sees a joker, he or she must immediately turn and walk away. Interestingly, the face cards and aces gravitate toward the center of the group. Number cards tend to stop talking as no one speaks to them. They walk around the outer edges of the group and don't talk. Their actions say, "Why should I talk when no one is going to talk to me?" Jokers tend to go to the outside of the group and just stand watching. They do not like the activity and hope it will end shortly. This activity demonstrates how most schools interact with groups of educators and students. The aces and face cards represent the "Royal Family." The number cards and jokers represent those who do not feel they are an important part of the school community. The participants who are aces and face cards experience popularity, recognition, importance, pride and connectedness. Number cards and jokers feel isolated, disrespected, invisible, and are a non-caring participant.

Your school community is divided into the somebodies and the nobodies: Between the Royal Family versus the common people that have no sense of importance. Schools tend to focus on the elite athletes and scholars and not on all stakeholders. Imagine coming to school everyday having people turn their back on you, not being respected for your gifts and talents, or being told that your accomplishments are not worthy when compared to the accomplishments of other groups on your campus.

Imagine being one of the number-card students in this deck who find themselves alone in a corner, hiding in a hallway during the lunch period, or not having anyone with whom talk to all day. There are students on your campus that are just like these students. Some are even suicidal. Some need you dearly. For some, you're all they have. By expecting that all students are gifted and talented, and by providing the chance for students to be successful at something, you allow them to break free of the number that they have been dealt. When there are more opportunities for success, and you expect and celebrate more types of success, more students get to experience being part of the family instead of feeling like an outsider. At the World's Greatest High School, the key is to expand our definition about what gifts, talents, and skills are worth noticing. We then expect more great things from students because we are looking for more types of success. Can you imagine what life would feel like for students who were finally noticed for being successful at something, and being expected to do more great things? Making "everybody a somebody" could change your school.

Value #5: Everyday is an opportunity to become the World's Greatest Me.

At the World's Greatest High School, each person on campus expects to become a better version of "me" than the day before – and its members expect everyone to work purposefully together to develop each person's gifts, talents, and skills.

People in the World's Greatest High School are a lot like a rubber bands. If you hold a rubber band in the palm of your hand it has no power; it does not do anything. However, if the rubber band is stretched and then let go, it is propelled somewhere. Similarly, when each member of the World's Greatest High School is stretched to his or her edges, they are more likely to be propelled somewhere than if they simply sit still. Lots of schools suffer from *loose rubber band syndrome*. They don't stretch students, staff, and their communities in such a way that can propel them anywhere meaningful. Instead, they allow them to sit inert. At the other extreme, many schools stretch students as if they were all the same learner and some end up breaking under the stress. At the World's Greatest High School, the job of the school is to stretch each individual to their optimum maximum, and then release them into the world.

When Park was a young adult and being trained by his college baseball Coach John Scolinos, a value system was being communicated to him. Coach Scolinos stressed the importance of challenging oneself daily and being the best version of oneself one could be each day. He believed, "It is more important to be a big league person than to be a big league player." He told our team, "If you are going to hang out with the donkeys, you will end up being a donkey." Similarly, when schools communicate the importance of stretching all stakeholders to their maximum capabilities, they develop a culture of importance that challenges each person to be better than he or she was the day before. Each person must develop his or her gifts, talents, and skills to maximum levels today and every day. Each student must see "it's cool to be sixteen now, but ten years from now, it wont be cool to still be sixteen socially, emotionally, and intellectually." At No Hope High School, there is no stretching of any student. At Mediocre High, students are not stretched enough to make any major impact or are stretched in the wrong ways entirely. At the World's Greatest High School, each person is stretched to his or her capacity as a unique being each day. By getting students to develop their confidence and personal expectation that they are great, their school is great. By working hard every day "I'm going to become the World's Greatest Me," you are infusing your people and your school with the idea, "We don't do okay - we do excellence."

Value #6: Everything we do, we do with PRIDE.

At the World's Greatest High School, the school's expectation of "Greatness" is clear in everything it does.

Nearly every school has a list of words that describe the best, desired student behaviors. However, these words lack the definition that is required to create a common language of excellence on campus. Many schools attempt to create learning goals for their students campus-wide, but don't adequately define what they mean by the language used in these goals. "Perseverance" may be listed as one of the desired qualities of the students of your school, but each idea that each staff member has about what perseverance means may be characteristically different from one another. One staff member may regard perseverance as overcoming academic obstacles, where another may think this relates to the emotional qualities of the student. Also, different groups within your school may have different expectations. The English Department may have a list of expectations, while the Math Department and

Softball team may have separate lists entirely. Without a common language around expectations, there simply are no clear expectations at all.

Many schools at which we have worked have talked about how students are expected to complete a "rigorous" program of classes. "Rigor" is a word that is much thrown around the edu-sphere. However, as we have visited schools throughout the country, we have noticed each school and staff member have differing opinions about what "rigor" means. One person regarded rigor as having each student taking difficult coursework with the expectation that they would pass these courses. Another staff member (along with much of the counselling department and administrative staff) took rigor to mean, "Well, if you don't pass this one, we'll allow you to try again a few times and if that does not work, we'll send you to adult school to complete the lowest needed class to graduate." When words used have multiple definitions, then the words have little concrete meaning at all. The potency is lost and results do not follow. Why call your school a school of "champions" when 25% of them don't graduate on time, 45% of them have to retake multiple core classes, and the average GPA for the school is a "C"? Clear definition is needed in the expectations you hold for your students, staff, and community members alike.

At the World's Greatest High School, our common language communicates the expectations that we hold for every member under our roof and connected with campus. All that we do communicates these expectations clearly. We work carefully to define what we expect, mean what we expect, and then we communicate consistently that what we expect is the norm. Further, having clear expectations allows us to truly celebrate accomplishment, because a student, staff member, or community member fulfilled the expectation at our school that success is the norm. Create clear expectations, mean them, and communicate them. Celebrate when people fulfil those expectations.

Summary

Expectations are the most basic roadmap of student, staff, and community member behavior at the World's Greatest High School. When you agree to and communicate a set of expectations stating that success is the norm, a common language develops that supports all you do under your roof. The expectations we hold of others often plays out in their actions. Create a place where the expectations are high, each person is stretched to their personal limits, and where "success" is the absolute expectation and success is clearly defined.

Blueprint Questions:

1. How will you show that you have high expectations for each person at your school?
2. How will you show everyone concerned that you actually mean "each person"?
3. What are some ways in which you can teach the people connected to your school that great things are expected for and from them?
4. What are some expectations that educators say they have about student behavior, but don't actually mean it?
5. What is one word that you want to define what is expected of students at your school? Do others believe in the same word? How do you know?
6. What actions would show a student, staff member, or community member fulfilling the expectation set by that one

word? How do you know when an expectation has been fulfilled?

Dares:

1. When you hear a staff member stating they have an expectation they will probably not consistently hold, call them on it and ask them for the "real" expectation.
2. Sit down with your staff or in small groups and write down the top words that you think should define what is expected of students, staff, and community members.
3. Write a common language of the top expectations you have about student and staff success with some clear definitions. Create an acronym from these.
4. Celebrate publicly when someone fulfills those expectations.

World's Greatest Mentors

Chapter 5

"No one gets anywhere without a mentor."

We have been teaching for years how "Mentors" (yes, a capital M) made the difference for us as developing educators - and human beings on a journey toward becoming "the World's Greatest Me." There were key people within each of our lives that shaped who we became, the roads we chose to walk down, and the paths upon which we were encouraged to keep on pressing, even though we sometimes wanted to run in retreat. We even acknowledged many of these Mentors at the front of this book because we would not be writing this without them. Thinking back upon those that have been such a paramount force in our lives, one of us would probably not be a teacher if it were not for a Mentor who was there at a key moment in our personal development. As in life, at school, Mentors play an integral role in the development of each person connected to your campus. This chapter is dedicated to exploring how Mentors can play a part in your building of the World's Greatest High School.

From the start, let's make the most important distinction regarding mentorship at the World's Greatest High School. You may be thinking right now, "How do I network students with mentors?" Instead, you should be asking the key question in regards to Mentors: "Who are my Mentors today?" Through this chapter, we will be making the case that not only is it vital that each student and parent gets the mentorship that he or she needs to become the World's Greatest Me, it is one of the World's Greatest shifts to focus upon *who mentors each staff member*, alongside *who mentors each student*. It is the mark of a great school that mentors its students, especially when other students are doing the mentoring. The gold standard, however, is when both students *and* staff are mentored by key people within their lives who can make the difference. Who are these Mentors? Read on and you shall see.

Value #1: We are what we believe – what we believe unifies us.

At the World's Greatest High School, we know that our beliefs are greatly influenced by those who have come before us and those that are seen as the sages within our tribe – our Mentors.

Every group in the world has its wise wizards, seasoned generals, and shamanistas. The community looks to these elders for guidance about how to be within each season of life within the school. At the World's Greatest High School, Mentors hold a very unique seat; they are able to set a standard for what is expected from their peers, students, parents, and the community. The important question is: do you give your Mentors the opportunity to sit in this seat of power?

In one of our recent videos that we sent to our email subscribers, we identified one-hundred-fifteen Mentors, the most influential high school Activities Directors in the State of California – and asked them, "What are the top characteristics of your leadership approach at your high school?" The results highlighted why Mentors are so important to creating a World's Greatest culture at your school. Nearly all Activities Directors described how their mentorship simply involved them being seen by others as being influential, inspirational, and a good role model. All they had to do to make a huge impact on unifying the school's culture was to be seen doing what they already do best. Shaping the powerful belief systems at your school can be as simple as showing off what your leaders are already doing.

In building your World's Greatest High School, the first step is to recognize those who are already the Mentors in your community. To whom do people *already* look for guidance and leadership? Second, provide them with the opportunity to be seen doing what they already do best. You may showcase their work, ask them to teach a skill at a staff meeting, or recognize and celebrate them publically. Finally, create a way where people meet with these Mentors in an intimate setting, such that bonds, friendships, and relationships can form.

Your students can be Mentors to your staff as well. At the World's Greatest High School, Park made it a point to have students teach the teachers the traditions of the school. When new staff members would join the school, the students would lead an orientation where the traditions were taught. Students also mentored fellow students in discovering what it meant to be part of this school family. Mentors are a chief means by which the campus is unified.

Value #2: All students have futures.

At the World's Greatest High School, Mentors believe that every person on campus has a future; also Mentors recognize that they have the ability to greatly impact the futures of others.

There are many people that you may know, including yourself, who might say that having "nay-sayers" in their lives has helped them become all they could be. These people claim that all the negative energy around them allowed them to excel because they had a foe to fight – namely, others' disbelief in their potential. What happens, though, for the student who only hears the statements of naysayers? What happens if there is not a single voice in their lives that is saying, "I believe that you can do this; I believe that you are capable and have great things ahead of you"? In a recent online video campaign, millions of students were reached by the message, "It gets better," there is promise later in life, regardless of your circumstances today. If you think that your students do not need such a message, consider that this campaign reached millions upon millions of students within the United States alone. Could it be that your students need to hear the message from a Mentor, "A future is not only possible, it's guaranteed" - and, what's more, that the future has great opportunity for them?

Educators also need to hear this message. One of the startling phenomena that we have seen in schools is the way that veteran teachers often find themselves on the outskirts of the social-sphere of campus. Because no other role is given purposefully to them, they have become the naysayers, or "not-sees," who put down any attempt to change the school. One school in which we worked began intentionally reaching out to such teachers to give them a role on campus, placing them with younger teachers who were in need of mentoring. A circle of support was built for these staff members as meetings turned into hangout sessions off campus, and these turned into deep friendships that began to unify the school. Do you know of a few educators on your campus who could benefit from the message that not only do they have a future, but they are integral to the futures of other educators?

When you don't bring people into the school family through mentorship, you leave them on the fringe. Outliers can often become outlaws. During Park's first year running school activities, he moved around the furniture in the staff lounge. There was such an opposition to change of any kind among the disconnected, disgruntled staff members that they all banded together to complain and attempted to get the Principal to fire Park - over moving a few couches. When you leave staff members without points of connection - or when you allow the wrong connections to fester, rotten things can happen. When you purposefully create opportunities for mentorships and the right kind of friendships to form, the results can be heartening.

In short, at the World's Greatest High School, we know that Mentors are a chief way by which the belief that "all students have futures" is communicated to kids. Mentors are also a way by which educators are cared for and celebrated for their vital role on campus.

Value #3: No one gets anywhere without a teacher.

At the World's Greatest High School, educators recognize that no one gets anywhere without a Mentor and that the impact of Mentors is exponential.

Think about one educator in your life who had a profound impact on you as a human being.

Can you think of someone who had a similar impact that was not an educator? Nearly everyone has had the benefit of a person in their lives that shifted their thoughts, feelings, or behaviors to a new place. We know that Mentors have an immense power that not only deserves honor, but requires our focus as well. At the World's Greatest High School, Mentorships are not left to be "chance meetings," like those that we experienced as young educators. Instead, Mentors and mentees are given the opportunity to meet up, spend time with one another, and transmit the values of the World's Greatest High School between them. This is not about creating rigid table-groups at your next faculty meeting or assigning one staff or student to another for "mentorship." This is about creating ways by which staff and students can organically meet and build these Mentor-mentee relationships on purpose.

At one school at which we worked recently, we spoke to a young teacher, Gary, who was in his fifth year in the profession. We asked how Mentors had impacted him. There were many things that we gleaned from this conversation that affirmed what we already knew: No one gets anywhere without a Mentor, and Mentors have exponential impact upon the school community. Gary described that after his first two years teaching, he was strongly considering leaving the profession altogether. After spending nearly ten hours per day on campus planning for classes, teaching, and being part of co-curricular activities, he found that he was exhausted and receiving little recognition for his hard work. One day, he came to school to find, what he considered the ultimate insult: His room assignment had changed mid-year without any prior warning. He arrived to campus to find his desk on a custodial cart headed across campus. He said he nearly walked off the job that day. A few weeks later, after tempers had calmed down, one of his staff neighbors walked in during lunch and asked if he could eat inside his room. This started a powerful mentorship between Gary, a young teacher, and Robert, a senior teacher who had been at the school for nearly twenty years. Gary told us that it was this mentorship that allowed him to stay in the classroom as a teacher; the relationship also encouraged him to start a mentorship program on his campus for other new teachers. Now this school is a model for teachers mentoring teachers.

What makes the role of Mentors so important? At the World's Greatest High School, it is often the Mentors that transmit the value system of the school to new members. By taking younger, less experienced family members under their wings, staff can mentor staff, students can mentor students, and parents can mentor parents about what the school is all about and how this place is the best place to become the World's Greatest Me. So, as we acknowledge the power that Mentors hold, we can start creating ways by which these Mentors can meet with those who are in the most need at your school. Will you make this a priority for this year? Can you see, how for some, Mentors can make or break them being part of your school or dropping out?

Value #4: All students are gifted and talented.

At the World's Greatest High School, Mentors seek out and celebrate the gifts, talents, and skills that each person brings into the school.

How much time does the individual teacher have to figure out the individual gifts, talents, and skills of each student? How about of fellow staff members? If everyone at your school has some unique set of gifts, talents, and skills that they can offer your school, Mentors are one of the chief means by which these are discovered and used. Mentors have the ability to recognize innate qualities in their mentees that are often unseen by others. It's through the deep relationship that mentors develop with their mentees that hidden gifts proudly emerge over time. In an environment where being skilled or notable is scary and undesirable, it is through the caring attention of a mentor that the courage is developed to bring one's gifts into the light. All that is required is that you allow Mentors and mentees to spend time with one another, and the gifts, talents, and skills will emerge naturally. Will you provide opportunities such as these?

Think about a mentor in your life who has enabled you to see more of yourself than you saw before. Sara, one of the Activities Directors at a model school in Northern California, is an expert at finding the unique facets and qualities of her leadership students that will benefit the team as a whole. What is unique about her way of mentoring is that she mentors students one-on-one, and she puts students in a position to mentor one another within her program. The result is that the value system of her school is transmitted from her, to her students, between her students, and to the community at large. Among many accomplishments, this has allowed her school, through her mentorship, to earn a world record as the most successful food drive at that time. Through her mentorship and the resulting mentorships between students, her community banded together in a way that would not have been possible otherwise. By creating a network of mentorships, the gifts, talents, and skills of all can not only assist the individual students, staff, parents, etc., they can also assist the community at large collectively.

Hence, at the World's Greatest High School, it is through mentorships that gifts, talents, and skills are discovered. All that is required is that you allow mentorships to take place, and encourage them in such a way that allows for such self-discovery, affirmation, and transmitting of the World's Greatest Values. Often, what sets mentorships into motion is simply educating the people within your school that mentorships matter and that they are easy to start. Will you hand your staff, students, and parents the tools to start mentoring one another? Sometimes, the only "tool" that is required is the ability to meet someone and share a bit about one's life experience.

Value #5: Everyday is an opportunity to become the World's Greatest Me.

At the World's Greatest High School, each person seeks to become a better version of "me" than the day before - and Mentors work purposefully to develop each person's gifts, talents, and skills.

Have you ever exercised and been frustrated about the lack of results? Often, it is through our own eyes we see the least progress along our path of becoming the best "me." However, if you have had the benefit of working with a coach, you have probably experienced the affirmation of being "one step better" than the day before. Mentors not only transmit the value of being the World's Greatest Me every day, they are also able to mirror back the accomplishments that have been made along the way. Mentors play an important role by simply observing and telling those they mentor how far along they have come. Quite literally, Mentors and mentees develop a shared language of accomplishment as they both develop themselves into better versions of themselves.

During Park's college baseball years, not only was Coach developing Park each day into a better version of himself, Scolinos was also transmitting a value system and way of speaking about accomplishment as well. He used story and metaphor, such as describing each day as "stretching the rubber band tight for power," and not being "like the fly bouncing on the same spot on the glass." Coach taught his mentees how to speak about becoming a better human being and gave them clear guidance about what to do along the way. Mentor-mentee relationships become very personalized. They are not something that can be thrown together once per month at your staff meeting or once a year at freshman orientation; mentorships are something worth fostering and emphasizing intentionally, consistently, and strategically.

Thinking about the "story" of your school, think about the names that come up therein. What were the roles of these people in assisting the school in becoming what it is today? If you find yourself recounting the negative descent of the school into turmoil, then clearly Mentors would benefit you immensely. However, if you are one of the fortunate schools that can chart the ascent of the school to the level of greatness it possess today, chances are you have much to say about the people that had a hand in building your World's Greatest High School one brick at a time. How do you honor these people? How, where, and when do you celebrate the successes they create and support? How do you continue to allow them to be part of each person at your school becoming the World's Greatest Me? Are you ignoring them or allowing them to be celebrated? This brings us to the final World's Greatest Value in regards to Mentors.

Value #6: Everything we do, we do with PRIDE.

At the World's Greatest High School, the school's one-of-a-kind culture of "Greatness" is clear in everything it does.

Mentors are the chief transmitters of the World's Greatest Values. They have the single most intimate relationship with those with whom they mentor as teachers, peers, and allies. Mentors, then, are also the keepers of the culture in a major way on your campus. What happens when your Mentors are not connected to the one-of-a-kind culture of greatness at your school? Or, more appropriately, what if your school does not include the vital Mentors in its one-of-a-kind culture and leaves these people feeling "on the fringe"?

Like many campuses, yours may have "islands" or "camps" that center around specific educators at your school. Often, these mini nation-states are simply a product of the mentorship that these educators provide. They are not directly connected to the larger mission that your school is undertaking, but they serve a purpose of importance nonetheless. For example, at one school at which we consulted, a stellar math teacher had an entire math academy set up to serve his students. The academy was connected to a local college and served hundreds and hundreds of students during his tenure as teacher. What was missing was the inclusion of this educator in campus-wide decisions about the school's culture of greatness. This educator was so excluded from important conversations that he simply took matters into his own hands - and, to his well-deserved credit, he created something that served students like no other program on campus. What happened, however, when he retired? The program that he had worked so hard to create died. Because the school failed to connect with this educator-Mentor and the amazing work that he was doing, all that he had created turned to dust when he was no longer tending it each day. How much benefit are your Mentors creating on your campus today that would not continue if they stepped away? How could you include them and what they are doing for your community into the "what's great" about your school? When you celebrate them and allow them to be part of decision making campus-wide, you enable their work to be school-wide and allow their work to live beyond them.

As a Mentor yourself, you could play a huge role in bringing together the major players or Mentors at your school. By having conversations with them about the amazing things that they are doing, you could come to consensus about how you can help one another accomplish the large goals that your campus has set together. In short, by purposefully seeking out those that are already mentoring at an amazing level, you can have them assist you in building your World's Greatest High School. Will you reach out to them?

Summary

Mentors are any staff, student, parent, or community member that assists in transmitting the World's Greatest Values to others at your school. Mentors are also those that assist your school community in discovering the gifts, talents, and skills that are developing through their work at the World's Greatest High School. You have the ability to create opportunities for Mentors to meet mentees regularly and intentionally, knowing that the power of these relationships is truly one-of-a-kind. The power of Mentors is exponential, as it is through mentorship that others begin to mentor others and so on. One Mentor can impact thousands of people. Mentors already exist on your campus, so have them take part in what you are doing in creating the World's Greatest High School. Mentors allow their mentees to be included daily in the vision of the World's Greatest High School. When you mentor others, remember you have limits. Consider developing the strength of one person around you in an effort help them grow. You have immense power already - all you have to do is take your seat as a Mentor and help others do the same. Don't shy away from who you are!

Blueprint Questions:

1. Who are the major Mentors at your school today? Can you name students, staff, parents, and community members?
2. Who are some people on your campus that you feel would make amazing Mentors if given the opportunity?
3. How does your school encourage and enable students to mentor students?
4. How does your school encourage and enable staff to mentor staff?

5. How could you reach out to make someone feel important?

Dares:

1. Ask a senior teacher to take a new teacher out to lunch. You pay for it.
2. Have your older leadership students meet with specific underclassmen throughout the year.
3. Put student, teacher, and community member heroes at the center of events that you hold. Allow these Mentors to transmit their stories and values to the larger group. Give them a microphone.
4. Learn the gifts of one student and plug them into an outlet for those gifts.
5. Say "hello" and shake the hand of a new student each day.
6. Write a hand-written note once per day on assignments, congratulating a student about a way in which you saw them grow.

World's Greatest Relationships

Chapter 6

"Each one of us has immense value. When we work together, our value multiplies. When the whole school is working together, our value grows exponentially."

When we talk about building, maintaining, and further cultivating relationships on campuses throughout the United States, it's common for us to hear a snicker from an audience member. Some have said, "Yeah right, Park, come see the kind of mess we've got going on! You think you've seen feuding - come to our school!" In reality, we have seen some pretty crazy dysfunction in terms of interpersonal relationships between staff members, students, parents, and community members. In fact, this trend of debilitating relationships within schools is so bad that an entire movement of education reform has sprung forth from it; this movement is dedicated to getting teachers out of their silos to start talking again. So many of us in education have been alone in our rooms for so long that we have forgotten how to get out and fruitfully communicate. At the World's Greatest High School, there is a systematic way in which the school cultivates relationships between everyone within. It's not the last thing that is done - it is the first. In this chapter, we're going to tell you how you can go about doing this in a way that infuses the World's Greatest Values into your high school, one conversation at a time.

Value #1: We are what we believe - what we believe unifies us.

At the World's Greatest High School, our beliefs influence us to put relationships at the core of all that is done on campus.

Your school's beliefs about the value and role of relationships is as easy to see as the number of people in the teacher's lounge; the number of minutes allocated for "common planning"; and the way in which offices, classrooms, and commonspaces are arranged. High schools were originally built on a collaboration model of top-down, hierarchical businesses like factories. There was a principal at the top who would delegate tasks below him or her. People were organized into departments of like subjects. Little discussion was fostered between these groups. Students were likewise organized by grades. Accordingly, social spaces within schools were also organized in segmented areas, where little was centralized besides the front office. Time and space for collaboration, therefor, was also placed into tight, neatly organized slots. Many schools have not moved on from there. Some schools even have actual regulations against having couches - we're not joking here. Collaboration is often something that happens in small, pre-planned slots that just barely fit into the instructional day. On some campuses, it simply does not happen at all. Think about the ways in which the people at your school get together inside planned meeting times, on the spur-of-moment, and when school is not even in session. This says a lot about the beliefs that your school has wrapped up in this huge area of importance - relationships.

The reason that relationships are so key is that they are the transmission system for your school's values. When students talk to one another, educators interact with their peers, parents and community members enter the mix, and when then they all start talking and doing some part of life together, they interchange the value system of the World's Greatest High School to each other. Peoples' lives can be entirely transformed, simply by the value system of the

World's Greatest High School being transmitted to them. These values are so empowering because they say, "your value is my value."

Relationships empower. One of Park's students at the World's Greatest High School was Mike, who was a shy, often-bullied student; Mike had immense potential, but he would rarely show it because of the way that others perceived him. It was through his relationship with an educator, Park, that Mike was able to walk into the student store and say, "Hey Mr. Park, I think that we could totally make this place work better if we simply put the register over here, put up displays here, etc." Starting with this first conversation, Mike pretty much ran the student store for three years. Because of the relationship that he had with Park, he was empowered by his teacher to use his skills in ways that would not be used otherwise. Mike was able to use his gifts, talents, and skills in a meaningful way because of his relationship with Park; without this, his entire high school career would have been entirely different. Mike was placed in a position where he could be developed. Park was able to infuse the World's Greatest Values into Mike as they worked together. Today, Mike is the CEO of a highly successful firm. When relationships empower, the people involved are more and more able to transmit the values of the World's Greatest High School and become the World's Greatest Me.

Park had the benefit of having the kind of relationship with his administrators that empowered. Years ago, the principal of the World's Greatest High School sat across Park at her desk patiently as Park was enthusiastically describing what he was planning for the school. He was excited, but also looking for approval from his administrator. He had plans on paper. He had so much to say and show. About five minutes into Park talking about what he wanted to do for the school, she leaned across the desk and said, "Excuse me, I need to interrupt you." Park was dumbstruck. She looked at him in the eye and said, "Do you expect me to do *your* job?" Park was mortified. What she was saying was, "You are the Activities Director and I trust you." Park was caught so off guard, he did not know what to think at the time - but eventually saw that this principal had his back completely. They had the type of relationship that said, "I empower you fully to go do your job and be the best you can be. Your success is our success."

As you are building the World's Greatest High School, begin by looking at where relationships happen and do not happen on your campus. Where are walled-up fortresses where people don't talk with one another? Where do the students who are not plugged into safe, positive relationships congregate? What is the school already doing to assist with building relationships that allow the value system of the school to be shared? If relationships could occur, where on campus would they physically occur? Second, build one space to hold one specific type of relationship. No, this does not necessarily mean going out and constructing a building for these purposes; it probably involves you could hold an event! If you want freshman students to be able to interact with one another, create a space for them to do that. If you want staff to have relationships, build a comfortable, clean, food-filled place in which they can collaborate and build such relationships. Finally, start thinking about how the values of your school can be transmitted via the relationships that you intentionally build for the school. What will the relationships that you start planting on campus say about what the school believes? If the only relationship that happens is at set common planning times, what does that say about what the school believes regarding the value of relationships and collaboration? It all starts by putting people in a place where they can fuel each other and transmit the value system of the school between them.

Value #2: All students have futures.

At the World's Greatest High School, people work with one another to create a new future that was not possible when they were flying solo.

Why is it that homeless kids who are living in their cars are sometimes able to survive and thrive in high school, while some students from seemingly picture-perfect life experiences fail? How is it that staff members who have experienced painful life events are still able to be some of the most valued teachers on our staff? How can a community who has undergone major hardship still embody such potential? The answer to these questions: Relationships create possibilities for futures that could not exist with individual persons living their lives alone. Interpersonal relationships on your campus form a mandala of promise that rests not on one individual. They create a network of support that holds the values of the World's Greatest High School always within heart's reach allowing the community members to overcome difficult circumstances. "The future," and hope for the future, is something in which people can believe.

These futures actually can come true because so many people are working together to build them. Will you create such a network on your campus?

One of the marks of great schools is the way in which educators continue the dialogue about "what's working" for students and fellow staff outside planned collaboration hours. Schools often struggle with dialogue because they cut off Facebook and other social networking sites from their computers. Sadly, this restricts access to the place where much conversation is happening. For example, one school at which we visited had entire "off the books," "off the server" teacher conversations happening during school hours (in spite of school board policy against teachers using mobile devices) on private Facebook groups relating to what strategies educators were using in their classrooms. However, two educators at this school lamented that they could not institutionalize this social network use because of the rules against its use. How ironic that more conversations were happening online every day about their school than could EVER happen in a single day in the staff lounge. We often say in education, "if people would just collaborate... blah blah blah," but then we act surprised when people aren't talking in the limited ways we *allow* them to do so. Our position is: Allow teachers access to social networks. While we have your attention, we also think texting amongst teachers is a good thing too. When you open your school conversation in the places in which people actually are already talking, conversation usually expands into other arenas. Expand physical social spaces on campus while lifting restrictions on virtual communication. How can you foster more conversations about futures? Make more spaces for conversation.

If people are not talking about futures - then it often feels like there is no future. The first step to building relationships is to consider where the conversations are already happening at your school - often in spite of the rules and systems that we have put in place to control such conversations. Then, it is important to start thinking about what roadblocks we have put in place to silence or mitigate conversation. Did we take out the couches from the staff lounge? Do we no longer have that free coffee pot hanging out somewhere? Did we take away the staff lunch window and began asking staff to cut in line in front of students? Finally, we want to start building new conversation spaces wherein teachers can talk about the great things that they are doing and that their students are doing inside and outside of school. No, this is *not* a brag-board on the office wall. Instead, create places in which people like to sit down for a few minutes. When you create such spaces, you open up chances for the conversations that are going to enable futures to happen. Here's the kicker though: it's really as easy as letting your best teachers do what they are doing already. Seek them out and see what they are doing: chances are, they are already fostering such relationships.

Value #3: No one gets anywhere without a teacher.

At the World's Greatest High School, educators recognize that no one gets anywhere without a teacher and that the impact of teachers is exponential.

Teachers are already creating conversation centers on your campus. Their rooms are the social spaces of champions. From students, to staff, to happy and disgruntled parents alike, people come to teachers' rooms to have lunchtime conversations and after school hang-out sessions. Walk around campus after hours and you'll notice that there are often many cars in the parking lot. Track down these people and you will probably find at least a handful of others hanging out with them in their classrooms. Often, when students hang out with teachers in this way, teachers are able to advocate for these students in ways that would not be likely otherwise - all because the relationship was present.

Bethany was one of Park's students who wanted to go to West Point. During her early years at the World's Greatest High School, she was not doing well academically; however by the time she was at the end of her sophomore year, she was beginning to pick up significant traction. Her goal of going to West Point was definitely within reach. Bethany's stepdad, however, saw otherwise. He believed that going to West Point was an unlikely future for his stepdaughter. His negativity and hostile questioning of Bethany was having a major influence upon her. "Does she really have what it takes?" he would ask Park. Because Park had developed the relationship with Bethany through the time they were spending together with other students, Park was in a position to advocate for her in an informed way. "Absolutely, she has what it takes," Park told her stepdad. Today, Bethany is a West Point graduate and holds a high rank in the Army. Without an advocate, she may have never attained the grand future that she wanted for herself.

Start thinking about what ways in which teachers are *already* positioning themselves to be advocates for fellow peers, students, and parents at your school. Which teachers step into the forefront of conversations about people-in-need on a regular basis? How do these teachers go about finding out whom needs what? Where are the conversation centers on your campus? When you put educators in the position to be advocates for others, amazing things start to happen. Namely, these educators are able to do what they already do best - reach out and cultivate a relationship that creates the potential for a future that would not have existed otherwise. Educators have the ability to point to something within others that is notable and worthy. All you have to do is to further provide the means for them to build such relationships and praise those that are the advocates on your campus.

Value #4: All students are gifted and talented.

At the World's Greatest High School, educators seek out and celebrate the gifts, talents, and skills that each person brings into the school.

It's through relationships that gifts, talents, and skills are often discovered. Without the relationships, the talents can still emerge, but they are not captured as quickly and accurately. When someone who has a relationship with us points to us and says, "That! That is something in which you do well!" our perspective toward that thing shifts into a mode of possibility. Think about the students who sit in your classrooms today. What happens when an educator points out a skill at which they perform well? These students begin to think differently about this skill than ever before. They begin to place emphasis on it. Eventually, it becomes a gateway for other opportunities, just because someone paid a little attention to it initially. What happens, then, when an educator *purposefully* develops that skill for that specific student? When educators become the coaches of their peers, students, parents, and community members, building each individual skill for each individual person, exponential possibility is at hand. What happens next is quite surprising: People begin transmitting this message of possibility to one another. When you allow students to be the source of knowledge and inspiration, they become beacons of success for one another.

Mazzy was a flabby, flakey, excited young student who had a huge passion and vision for making people feel welcome and celebrated at school. She was initially Park's student body Vice President, and she was promoted to President during the school year at a very young age. Her drive and bubbly personality would draw out the best in her entire class. Park would push her and her class hard to make a difference on campus. Not only did Park know her individual strengths and weaknesses, but he sought to develop these uniquely for her as his student. Because he knew her so well, he was able to advocate for her – which upped her game as a young student government president to a level that the school had not previously seen. When you talk to her today, she talks about how "Parkhouse would kick your butt if you were not performing to your potential." This caused her and her class to reach new heights as a school that would not be possible if they did not have an advocate. The talents of students, staff, parents, and community members are enhanced by relationships with advocates.

At the World's Greatest High School, we draw attention to those within our community who are already changing the game for students, staff, and parents. We celebrate them. People begin to realize the power that they hold through relationships – seeing these not solely as friendly hang-out times, but also places where people are challenged to become the best versions of themselves.

Value #5: Everyday is an opportunity to become the World's Greatest Me.

At the World's Greatest High School, each person on campus seeks to become a better version of "me" than the day before – and its members work purposefully to develop each person's gifts, talents, and skills.

When people are becoming the "best" of themselves alongside others doing the same, the growth experienced is exponential. Like many in the education space, we've noticed that teachers hiding away in their classrooms for extended periods of time is often the norm. When teachers get together and start talking about teaching, teaching is often impacted. However, when people are hurting, lonely, angry, and hungry from something they don't have, talking about teaching strategies can only have so much impact upon the school community. What would happen if more time was spent enabling each other to be better, happier human beings – as well as better teachers? How would the way people teach shift if they had more of what they wanted in life? How would learning be impacted if more students were experiencing brighter futures each day at your school? How would parents react if they could tangibly feel that life was getting more and more fruitful by the minute? When the feeling of possibility shifts, behavior often follows. When an individual's behavior supports new possibilities, his or her life is changed. When people work together to shift their lives, the gravity of opportunity enters a whole new dimension.

At the World's Greatest High School, people sharpen people. When Park's student, Mike, walked into the student store and began talking about how it could be improved, he was sharpening Park's ability to make a compelling shopping experience for his students. Simultaneously, Park was sharpening Mike's ability to follow through and tangibly bring changes into reality. Through their relationship, both Park and Mike - both teacher and student - were enhanced. They were able to become more and more the World's Greatest Me each day by working with one another. When you put people in the position of being able to advocated for one another, they have the ability to learn from each other and become better human beings. We have seen this play out in creative ways in student leadership teams from "accountability partners" to "personal coaches." We have seen teachers turn bland goals into deeply personal aspirations that they want to accomplish - not just about their teaching, but about their life as a whole. How could you make this brand of relationship more possible at your school? Could it be as simple as buying a few couches or brewing a $0.25 pot of coffee each morning?

Value #6: Everything we do, we do with PRIDE.

At the World's Greatest High School, the school's one-of-a-kind culture of "Greatness" is clear in everything it does.

In closing, think about what's great about your school. How do people work with one another to make it even better? Is this growth something that is already organically happening at your school? Are there ways that you could "get out of the way" or encourage this type of relationship to form? Overall, is there an expectation at your school that everyone is to perform at their individual World's Greatest level?

At the World's Greatest High School, Park was witness to how the band, football team, students in advanced academic classes, leadership team, and students, staff, and parents at school rallies all went with the expectation that they were becoming the World's Greatest Me at the highest levels. He saw how people held the expectation of excellence everywhere, because of the pervasive culture of Greatness that was shining throughout the school. What made all this possible was the relationships between the students, staff, parents, and community members and the transmission of the one-of-a-kind culture of greatness within the school.

Summary

Relationships are not the last things that are attended to at the World's Greatest High School: They are the first things. From mentors; to the individual advocating that happens between students, staff, and parents; to the large social gatherings where the school's World's Greatest Culture is clearly on display, relationships are the means by which the school transmits its value system from one person to another. Once you have started infusing the World's Greatest Values into your school body, teaching your culture of Greatness, you can then start building and celebrating the places and spaces within which relationships are thriving on your campus. By cultivating these relationships, your responsibility of building the World's Greatest High School does not sit solely on your shoulders. A network of Greatness simply needs to be sparked and supported by you.

Blueprint Questions:

1. What people and places tend to be the heart-centers of relationships and conversation at your school?
2. Who are largely or completely disconnected from relationships and conversation at your school?
3. What are some ways you could encourage "community" on your campus?
4. What are some ways that you need to simply "get out of the way?"
5. What is your relationship to your school's values, expectations, and beliefs?
6. Who teaches the culture to new members of your school? How?
7. How are the students expected to be part of the teaching of the school's culture?
8. How are you personally making strides

to enhance the lives and well-being of those who teach with you?

Dares:

1. Look online or locally at garage sales for used couches. Buy them (yes, even if you can't get reimbursed) and put three of them in your staff lounge - as long as the couches don't smell too bad.
2. Place a coffee pot in a public space in your school. Advertise.
3. Pair key Senior students with key Freshman students. Have them meet regularly throughout the year.
4. Embrace social media for staff members. If you're not ready for this, start the movement underground, while respecting the laws and rules that govern your school.
5. Discover and exploit multiple avenues of connecting staff, students, parents, and community and business partners with one another. Take as many opportunities as possible to have people spend time with one another.
6. Allow students to be the teachers of

culture at your school.

7. Leave no one sitting alone in his or her classroom without the knowledge that there are allies *already* wanting to be part of his or her life.

World's Greatest Planning

Chapter 7

"When you plan success for a few, a few will be successful. Kids tend to fulfill the expectations we have of them. When you plan with the belief that all kids have futures, they will fulfill that expectation to extremes."

What makes some schools successful in strategizing for student success and able to get results? What allows one English department to design their own student reader within three weeks, while it takes another English department three years to create a common rubric for a single essay? What allows one student government to be the architects of some of the most meaningful reforms a school has ever seen, while another simply stagnates in indecision and misbehavior?

So much of what we are hearing in staff development meetings relates to the goals that we set and the plans that we build to make those goals come true. *Goals* are such an area of interest right now in education that entire conferences are enacted simply to allow teachers the time to set goals and plan for the coming school year alongside other educators. So why do some schools create very successful plans that come true, while others seemingly can't? We've observed three major trends in schools that shed some light on the answer.

First, many people within schools begin planning with the wrong intention - to fix a problem. What would you rather do: Fix your constantly broken vehicle, or have the car of your dreams? Silly question, right? The mindset to which people bring to the task of "fixing" a problem is much different than the task of building the school of our dreams. Instead of sitting down with a problem focus, sit down with your team and imbue the intention of creating a future that you all truly desire. Newsflash: People don't like planning and carrying out plans for a future they don't want, in which they have little at stake, and about which they have very little passion. People will fight tooth and nail to get the future of their dreams in their hands. So, will you let them plan for such a future?

Second, we've observed that many people within schools don't have the resources at their disposal to fulfill the goal that they are setting out to complete. When you read that line, you probably thought of money, right? Actually, the resource that people within schools chiefly lack is the time and energy needed to carry out the stellar futures which they wish to plan. One school at which we consulted wanted to build a place where every English Language Learner was proficient; however, there is only so much time that they could dedicate outside the classroom to planning that kind of school-wide change. Their total staff development time totaled around twenty hours for the entire school year! So much time was spent talking about sexual harassment, uniform complaint procedure, and the endless stream of "invaluable information" that could have been communicated via email, that only a handful of hours were available within formal, scheduled common planning time to make things happen. Add in the fact that many of the staff members were parents of high school age students, and it becomes increasingly clear how lack of time and energy contributed to this one particular school's inability to reach their lofty goal. With the right amount of time and personal energy, much of what your school wishes to accomplish could come true. How will you assist your staff, students, parents, and community members with the time needed to plan and carry out their compelling desires for the future of your school?

Finally, many people within schools lack the mindset that would allow them success in the first place. We aren't psychics, but we have an uncanny ability to tell within a few minutes if members of a school will be successful in the plans they are setting. The key factor that we recognize is the words that they use regarding their plans and the process of planning. When we hear, "Yeah, I spent two hours filling out this plan *for the principal*" we notice a clear sign of lack of ownership. When we hear, "Yup, here is the plan. *We'll see* what happens," we notice how unsure the future seems for these plans. Finally, when we hear, "Here we go again with another year of goal setting," we recognize that there are long-running, unproductive patterns and cycles within the school. The mindset required to create a meaningful plan starts with building a compelling future that one cares about. Then it requires specific resources to make that plan possible. In the end, it also takes the resolve to own those plans and take ownership of the outcome. How do you build a sense of ownership into the fabric of the plans that your school makes? This chapter is dedicated to answering that question.

Here's how you can apply the World's Greatest Values to the plans that your school sets.

Value #1: We are what we believe – what we believe unifies us.

At the World's Greatest High School, we know that our beliefs greatly influence the plans we make and how we go about making them.

If your school is like the hundreds that we have visited, you probably have "common planning time" or "staff development" regularly scheduled for the purpose of getting together to plan. The names of these events seem to imply what they are intended to be. For example, common planning is about getting together and creating a plan together; staff development is about being developed as a staff in some regard and creating a common-space exchange to plan, discuss, and carry out a learning strategy or plan for our students. The question we have for you is: Do you believe that the way in which your school goes about planning and using this time, lives up to your ultimate potential? Chances are, the answer is: *no*. Our beliefs as a school greatly influence the way in which we go about planning and the plans that we make for those inside the World's Greatest High School.

School planning is all about your campus producing a very specific product, but what is this product? Consider that the product that your school is selling, quite literally, is "futures." Is your school selling the idea that success here is the norm and that futures of great promise await those that emerge from your doors? Instead, is your school selling the idea that success is limited only to a select few students and that not everyone here has a future? The plans that we make as a school speak volumes about what we believe regarding these futures that we are producing. To illustrate this point, consider the following story.

When Park was building the World's Greatest High School, his school had just opened up and the whole campus had a set notion of what school spirit looked like. Many of his students were quite proud of what they believed they had accomplished, as they would say, "We have such great school spirit here! We have more school spirit than any other school around." They had a belief about themselves and the future of their school – that they had some of the best school spirit around. While this was a great belief to have, it was inevitably very limiting for these students. They believed that they had reached the peak of spirit at their school, so their ideas about what they and Park could accomplish in student government were extremely limited. After the school had been open for only a couple of months, many of the staff and student believed that they "had arrived." Park recognized that these limiting beliefs were choking off the future that they were truly trying to accomplish – a future where every student on campus could be their best. The only way to allow these students to advance forward and create more spirit was to show them how limited their beliefs were. Park eventually got ten key students into a couple of cars and drove to a neighboring high school, which happened to be one of their chief rivals. With a video camera in hand, they interviewed student after student about how each felt about their school. They videotaped their rival school's rally and brought it back to their student government. With the eyewitness accounts of the ten students and the video of the rally, Park was able to show how the plans that the student government were making regarding school spirit were limited by their beliefs. The students saw in hazy, home-video clarity how much school spirit could actually be infused into the student body. Their eyes were opened and their plans began to change. What they saw challenged them to be better.

So, what does your school believe collectively about the following values? Consider how each belief can potentially limit or enhance your staff's ability to create meaningful plans for those inside your school. We are passionate in pointing out that the current norm of planning-for-planning sake actually prevents educators from getting the results they want. This is because plans are only useful if people actually care about them personally, and if they have the resources and capacities to accomplish them. At the World's Greatest High School, the first step in planning is bringing to light and acknowledging the over-arching beliefs that the school already has tied up in the subject at hand. Second, reality-test these beliefs against the World's Greatest Values. Do your current beliefs model the futures you are attempting to produce as a school? Finally, as you are setting plans, create ones that fulfill the values that you aspire toward, while ensuring that they are doable. If the plans you set are not currently within your ability, how could you make plans to enhance your ability to move closer to your goals? The plans you create together with other educators unify you. Make your plans meaningful and aspiring toward the qualities that you want to embody as a campus.

Value #2: All students have futures.

At the World's Greatest High School, educators plan so that every student has a future.

What happens when educators only plan for the success of a select few students? Much of the planning that we see happening within the school's walls is related to the students who are doing fine or fantastically - those who are making the grade. We've sat in open discussions between staff members during professional development meetings and have often heard statements like, "Well, not all of them are meant to go to college," "Not every student will pass," and "If they don't do the work, then they won't get the grade." Each of these statements relates to a belief that each staff member has about each specific student within their classes. Our question is: What gives an educator the right to be the judge, jury, and executioner of a student's future? Does any teacher ever really have the right to look at a student and say, "I've made the decision that you will never (ever) pass this course?" Similarly, what gives educators the right to plan for the success of only a select group of students? Clearly, teachers have a responsibility to evaluate student progress, which often results in being assigned a grade. However, teachers do not have the right to permanently deem a student a life-long failure.

Our definition of "success" needs to expand in education. Few people look at world-class musicians and athletes and consider their math proficiency. Chances are, you don't wonder about your physician's acuity in English Literature. Skills in these areas are absolutely important and vital - and EVERY student should be proficient in these. Still, is this the only measure that your school uses to determine "success?" When Park was a leadership teacher at the World's Greatest High School, counselors would place some of the most troubled students in his classes. Many of the students in his leadership classes were failing their courses and were not enjoying "success" by the usual definition held by schools. However, Park provided lots of opportunities within his program for students to enjoy success at many levels - not just in English and Math. For example, when he would gather his leadership class together to brainstorm for campus activities, he would zero-in and provide a space for the visionaries (who were often not doing great in other content areas) to plan, create, and celebrate. These visionaries could enjoy the success of putting together an amazing plan for an event. Then,

Park would provide space for the organizers and do-ers of the class to put the plans into motion. Lastly, he would provide space for the celebrators and spirited-partiers to be the face of the event. In all, he would provide a way by which each student was utilized for his or her individual talent - from planner, to DJ, to greeter, to artist, and beyond. He planned for the success of each student - not just one type of student. Students were expected to pass and excel at all their content level courses, but their performance in those classrooms was far from the only measure of success at his school.

At the World's Greatest High School, we provide multiple avenues for student success, and we create ways for individual students to be successful. When we are building the World's Greatest High School, we know that the purpose of our school is not to provide teachers jobs; it is to ensure that kids have futures, no matter who they are or where they are today. When we provide outlets for kids to utilize their talents such that they can experience success, this will propel them into success in other areas of their school life. What we have seen time and time again is that when an educator builds a place in which a student can experience success, the student's and the educator's lives begin intertwining in such a way that will allow the student to be successful in other avenues. Will you plan for a way for each individual student to experience some type of success?

Value #3: No one gets anywhere without a teacher.

At the World's Greatest High School, educators plan as if "no one gets anywhere without a teacher," knowing that the impact of teachers is exponential.

When we place students in the position of experiencing success in something, they build pathways to become successful elsewhere. Teachers place each student in a position that will allow him or her to experience success at the World's Greatest High School. Think about the teachers that had a profound impact upon you during your lifetime. Did they enable you to experience accomplishment in something through your relationships with them? During our lifetimes, we definitely have had the benefit of many Mentors that have put us in the position to experience achievement that we would not have had experienced without relationships with these esteemed teachers. What would happen to your school if every teacher reached out to one - just one student in his or her classroom and decided to help the student be "a somebody" at something? You would have hundreds of students at your school who were suddenly being mentored and developed in a skill. Often, we mistakenly only provide these opportunities to those students your school expects to "excel."

If your school is like most schools, much of your time is spent focusing attention on the *Royal Family*: the students who are "somebody's" already at your school. These are the students who are in the academic top ten percent, are on the homecoming and prom courts, are the top athletes, and are the most involved students. All eyes seem to be always on them. What happens to a student who is not in the Royal Family? When are the eyes on this student? If you are the bottom twenty percent of students in terms of academic achievement, or one of the misbehaving students on campus, plenty of eyes are on you as well - at the front office, in parent meetings, or in the detention hall. There is also a whole group of students who sit between your Royal Family, and your bottom twenty percent; these students are just "in the middle." These are the students that get very little recognition or attention anywhere. What would happen if your school made it a point for each staff member to each mentor one of these students at your school?

At the World's Greatest High School, we plan for students to be plugged in with educators who will advocate for them. The stories of accomplishment flow automatically as each educator begins to build up each student in a specific skill. Then, through their success, these students begin to experience other types of success on campus as well. There are many ways that you can do this at your school. First, make it a point for your teachers to choose one or two students "in the middle" and mentor them in a talent that this educator sees. Second, build opportunities within your individual classroom for your students to utilize these talents. Finally, allow students to experience the achievement that each talent is bringing into their lives and build ways by which they can start using these talents elsewhere on campus. When you plan for student success in this way, students can begin to experience that they are, in fact, gifted and talented in something. This success will then spread throughout their lives.

Value #4: All students are gifted and talented.

At the World's Greatest High School, educators seek out and celebrate the gifts, talents, and skills that each person brings into the school.

Walk onto many campuses and you'd think the only places in which students can be talented is in the classroom and on the football field. Too often, we plan for only one or two narrow types of skill on campus - one academic, one athletic. We only define academic skill an "A" or high standardized test score in a core subject area like, English, Math, History or Science. We limit our definition of athletic skill as running a football down the field. When we plan for such a closed set of talents that get our attention and our energy at our school, there are few opportunities for most students to express their gifts. Consider what the opposite scenario would look like. What would it look like for there to be a wide array of ways that each student could express his or her gifts, talents, and skills on campus? What would that kind of school look like? To create such a place, we have to plan to allow students to showcase their skills in varied ways inside and outside the classroom. If your students experienced success in one avenue, don't you think they would be more likely to experience it elsewhere?

Inside the classroom, we have to plan our lessons, assessments, and way of being with students such that we have the opportunities - and the eyes - to see students showcasing talents of many kinds. So often, the focus in our classrooms is given to those students who are doing the best or the worst in the class. However, when that student moves their grade from a 70% to an 80% we may pay little or no attention. Further, when we are solely focused upon grades, we may ignore that a student has utilized incredible resilience to sit in the desk in our classroom, shrugging off conflict at home, walking a considerable distance to school, and sometimes going for hours without food to simply be the student that performs at a "C" level. If we gave students the chance to shine in varied ways, and had the eyeballs capable of recognizing different types of talent and success, what would show through?

One teacher at a school we visited was frustrated how his remedial English class could not seem to understand metaphor and theme. At the end of the semester, students failed their film analysis essay miserably. In frustration, he asked one student, "Didn't you understand this? You were talking in class about the film like you understood the themes perfectly. What happened in your essay?" The student said to this educator, "If you gave me the chance to paint this instead of writing it, I could definitely show you that I understood this film!" So the educator did just that: He allowed his remedial students the choice of writing an essay or painting a visual of their understanding of the themes of the film. In the end, he was not measuring essay-writing skills – he was measuring theme-understanding skills. Because he got out of the way and gave the students different avenues by which to express the same skill (theme comprehension), students were able to utilize their existing talents (like the ability to paint) to show their understanding. Interestingly enough, this same teacher taught further regarding the essay, trained his students to write it, and was able to use the painting as a way to support the essay writing skill – all because he enabled students to use one existing talent to support another.

Similarly, outside the classroom, do you provide varied ways at your school for students to get "plugged in" to niches that allow them to showcase their gifts, talents, and skills? Do you provide the same chance for the champion soccer team to be on display as the champion football team? Do you have the band showcase its latest program at a staff meeting? Do you allow the Future Farmers of America (FFA) students the same opportunity? When success of all kinds becomes the focus, your Royal Family expands beyond just a few students. Your school begins to be a place wherein everybody can be a somebody. This is not because you "dumbed down" the curriculum to allow more students to meet the lowered bar of "proficient." When you allow there to be more than one type of success at your school and when you provide "look at me" moments for your students, you are allowing more students to utilize their existing skills in realizing the goals of your school's program. This advancement of your students' skill in one area, in turn, assists in advancing others.

When we plan for allowing students to show off their individual gifts, talents, and skills inside and outside the classroom, we open opportunities for students to develop themselves in these skills alongside the other skills. When educators utilize these students' existing skills as scaffolds for other emerging skills, students are stronger for it.

Value #5: Everyday is an opportunity to become the World's Greatest Me.

At the World's Greatest High School, each person on campus seeks to become a better version of "me" than the day before - and its members work purposefully to develop each person's gifts, talents, and skills.

Every educator in the public school system has been exposed to Individual Education Plans (IEPs) for students with special needs on their campus. These plans provide an immense service to the students upon which they focus, as goals and plans are set for individual capacities and needs for those specific students. Each student gets his or her own plan that is specially crafted for his or her unique needs. Don't all learners at your school also have unique needs, capacities, gifts, goals, and aspirations? Don't they all? What would it look like for your school to be a place where each person was developed uniquely as an individual learner? This is the heart of the "World's Greatest Me" philosophy - that each day can be a chance to be better than the day before, because educators see the individual gifts, talents, and skills of students and develop each of them individually to be one step better than the day before. Could you plan for this kind of personal development at your school?

When educators are intentionally placed in the position of being advocates for individual students, developing individual skills, students have the opportunity to become better than the day before. This is because these educators call for the students to begin thinking of "futures" in a different way than students previously thought possible. Educators have the ability to place students in the position of being open to possibility, unfettered by "what's doable" in the short term. Often, we forget that most of our students are, by definition, "kids," and kids have the ability to dream in ways that adults often shut down. When educators free up students to dream (which is being an advocate for a future not yet realized) and work with these students to make these dreams come true, students can become one step better each day until the day they arrive. In Park's leadership classroom at the World's Greatest High School, brainstorming sessions would always start with "don't hold anything back," and "anything's possible" planning. Students would talk about how they wanted to have fireworks at the Air Band (lip sync) performance. They suggested showcasing the Air Band champions at other school rallies,

and they even were able to go to their rival schools in other cities to show off at these rival rallies. At each of these rallies, boos would turn into cheers as the rival school celebrated the performers. Because of Park, placing students in positions to engage in open-ended, unrestricted dreaming, students were able to expand their talents in ways that would not have been possible in a closed-minded environment. Educators can begin developing each student in their individual skills by first planning to allow students the ability to dream freely about a task and giving them the liberty to make these big dreams happen. Simultaneously, educators can watch for the specific gifts, talents, and skills emerging in these students as they work and attend to developing one specific skill at a time.

In all, this commitment that the school makes to develop each member of its body as an individual, whether a teacher, student, parent, or otherwise, starts with educators making the personal promise to develop each student as an individual learner with unique gifts, talents, and skills. These educators understand that all that is required to change the life of a student is for them to be one step better than they were yesterday. Could you make such a promise?

Together, could your school have such a high aspiration?

Value #6: Everything we do, we do with PRIDE.

At the World's Greatest High School, the school community plans for their one-of-a-kind culture of "Greatness" to be clear in everything it does.

There's a pattern in schools of campus activities – inside and outside classrooms, being done on the fly. Sure, things are placed on the calendar ahead of time, but parent nights, testing preparation, rallies, and lessons can often be planned "just in time" for the event. Little is planned out ahead of time. As a result the feeling that these events are part of a larger whole is lost. Last minute planning sacrifices part of the greater vision of what your school is all about. To illustrate what we mean, think about the way in which the world's greatest theme park organizes and plans events. First, when you walk into an event there, it is clear that it is oozing with the values and flair that make this the most "wonderful place." Second, there is a clear connection between what happens at this event and all the other events that are happening elsewhere. For example, the events literally showcase all the great stuff that is happening in that place, from the people to the notable works that the theme park is known for. In other words, everything about the brand is on display! What would it be like to plan in this way? What would it be like to plan in a way that considers all that your school is about and infuses that into planning classroom activities, rallies, parent nights, and the like? Planning for the greatest place on Earth looks different than planning for "just another day" at Joe Doe High School. Why does it have to be so?

Park loves to survey the "front office brand" of every school he visits. Just in case he's visiting your school, you may want to read this paragraph carefully. The front office says a lot about your school! Just like the entryway to the world's most popular theme park or Nike headquarters, the front office is a place where "all that we are together" can be showcased in a concentrated punch. When your school is planning in such a way that it's one-of-a-kind culture is visible in all it does, you can easily see evidence of this: everywhere. Does your front office show evidence of your school infusing its one-of-a-kind culture into every aspect of campus? Can kids (or anyone else) walk into your office and say, "Wow! Look at all these amazing things that kids are doing here?" Does your front office showcase what success at your school looks like? Or, conversely, does your front office showcase the dusty plaque of district goals with pictures of a handful of successful students from many years past? Is your front office the hall of dead principals? Could you plan out your events and activities (in and out of class) in such a way that the essential flavor of your school was always present?

You have to plan for what "success" looks like for your school before you can plan how to show off "student success." The first step is to sit down with your staff, students, parents, and community partners and truly get to the heart of what "success" looks like. Is it a confining definition that only a few will be able to meet? Is success something broad and deep that transcends a single mark, test score, or sport? So many schools talk about "student success" without defining what that is! The second step is to plan in such a way that this vision of student success is showcased EVERYWHERE – at every event, in every classroom, in every plan that you create as a school. Show everyone that your school's product is the different types of success that your students, your staff, and your community are attaining. This idea of defining success as if it were a product that your school creates and sells is a new concept to many in education. The next chapter will focus specifically on this idea.

Summary

When you plan for creating success, rather than planning to fix problems, the way in which your school goes about doing what it does each day is revolutionized. First, we plan for the individual successes of students based upon their uniqueness as human beings. Second, we place students in a position to be mentored by educators who can advocate for them and their personal development. Third, we expand the thinking of our school regarding what success looks like, allowing educators to see that student success transcends a single aptitude or a cumulative GPA. Fourth, we build a place where each person has the chance to become a human being better than the day before. As your school develops its one-of-a-kind culture, attend to the one-of-a-kind definition of success that your school holds dear. Next, we'll talk about how to build that definition of success for your school.

Blueprint Questions:

1. As an educator, how do you know when an individual student has advanced his

or her unique skills? To what evidence do you typically look? What evidence do you typically ignore?

2. In what ways does your school treat students as "groups of kids," as opposed to "individual students?"
3. What are some examples of student success on campus that you don't often see being broadcasted or celebrated?
4. If you were to make an educated guess, what would be your schools unique definition of success?

Dares:

1. Each day, notice when you are looking at some of the work your students created. Choose one specific student and mention one skill that you saw them advance through an assignment, in a conversation, or elsewhere.
2. Make a list of what's great about your school, your students, and your community.
3. Using the list you created, highlight those "greats" that are often discussed

on campus. Consider which ones are rarely mentioned.

4. Celebrate that which you would like to see more often.

World's Greatest Branding

Chapter 8

"Is your one-of-a-kind school expressing itself in a one-of-a-kind way?"

How do you spread the message that your school is the World's Greatest place to become the World's Greatest Me? How do you emerge from being seen as No Hope High School or Mediocre High to the status of World's Greatest? Here's a better question: What is the most ignored facet of high schools that could create a huge impact - just simply by giving it a little attention?

The majority of our talks at conferences throughout the United States are about answering these questions. In addition to the topics that we have already discussed in this book so far, we always talk about branding. When we get to this part of the talk, usually happening about seven minutes into our presentation, there is always at least one person in the audience who gets this inquisitive look on his or her face and opens their conference program to make sure that he or she is in the right room. "Branding?" their face is saying. "What the heck does being a great school have to do with branding? What are we - a fast food chain?" This chapter is about answering these questions and talking about how branding is an area that can create great change for your school with just a little attention.

First, let's define "branding" to set the stage for why it is so vital for your school. *"Branding" is the feelings, names, symbols, and slogans used to identify a product.* Your branding represents your flagship product to the world at large. In fact, branding can be so successful at being your spokesperson that these names, symbols, and slogans often become as recognizable as the actual product itself. Think about golden curves over hamburgers, illuminated fruit on the back of your laptop, or an odd shape on the side of your shoes. These icons are immediately identifiable brands which so connected to the products that they represent that they communicate the emotions, ideas, and lifestyle that is attached to them. Similarly, a small green goddess on the side of your coffee cup says, "the best," simply by being there amongst the steam of your morning brew.

Branding identifies the products it represents by the power of association.

So what product does your school sell? Again, back at our conference presentation, people start giving us the stink-face when we ask this question. "Product?" their wrinkled noses say. "Do you mean in the student store?" Your school's product is the educational experience that your school creates for each student as well as the future that this educational experience produces. The use of your product, or a student's journey through the learning program at your school, produces a specific result; such as dropout, graduation with skill, or graduation with major skills lacking. Your graduates, or lack thereof, become the outcomes that use of your product creates. If graduation (or not) is the product, then what your students do in the world outside your school is the result of the use of your product. This mindset may involve a new way of looking at your school; many people are not used to thinking of what the school offers as a "product." As a result, schools often miss out on a huge opportunity to perfect their product and make the name of their school, their logo, their mascot, and all the regalia associated with the school mean something powerful in the community. Will you develop your brand such that your school's name means "World's Greatest" in your community? Or will you settle for "Mediocre High"? The choice is yours!

In regards to this piece of Building the World's Greatest High School, the key decision that every school has to make is whether they will first infuse the World's Greatest Values into their brand, such that the messages that are being communicated about the school are accurate. Do you think that your school today is being accurately portrayed in the community? This chapter is NOT about learning how to send messages about what your school does; it's about perfecting what your school does with the community and with the people associated with your school. This is about perfecting your product – not your commercials.

Value #1: We are what we believe – what we believe unifies us.

At the World's Greatest High School, we know that our beliefs greatly influence how our school brands itself.

As we have talked about in previous chapters, your school's collective beliefs are *already* clear in all it does. At all times, silent messages are sent by the school brand that surrounds your students, staff, and community. One school, for example, had rolling lawns at its entrance with a giant, marble sign with the school's name. It was gorgeous. Then, the school decided to place giant, barred security fences in front of these grass areas. Now, a large sign reads as you walk in "Such-n-Such High School is a CLOSED campus." Think about how the school's beliefs about being "secure" actually send silent messages quite to the contrary to parents, staff, and students. The message sent, if you talk to these people, is that this school is "locked up," "confining," and "a pain to get into!" While there is much merit to securing schools, it is also important to consider that the visuals which surround people every day, have a pretty impressive impact upon how they feel: Someone believes this is what "secure" looks like, while others feel this is what "trapped" looks like. Without even realizing it, this school branded itself as being "the prison" (as it is referred to by many alumni who remember the "grassy entrance" days), simply because it was unaware of how its beliefs about security were being broadcast in its visual brand. This story has played out in at least five schools we have visited.

When your school is aware of its beliefs about its brand and is intentional in shaping this brand to take up the values of the World's Greatest High School, your school can send immensely influential messages. These messages may come though simple avenues like having green grass, a well-painted sign, or a few smiling people standing around. Consider one of the most impressive models of how to show off your beliefs through your branding. When Park visited Nike Headquarters, he was in awe of how flawlessly they were able to show off what "they were all about" simply by having some displays and shoes hanging around. When Park walked in, he saw a giant image of Michael Jordan (their greatest champion at that time) with his shoes. When Park walked down the adjoining corridors to the lobby, he found row upon row of the various sports represented by this company, with pictures of their champions, and their shoes. All in all, by simply employing some posters and some slightly-used footwear, Nike is able to paint the picture that this is the place where champions reside. You are standing in a hall of heroes. Contrast this to how your school's beliefs about itself are on display in the front office, on the walls of the quad, or in the parking lot. Many schools that we visit are showing off the belief in these areas that "not much is going on here which is worth talking about." Even when you are not intending on sending a message, the absence of one is a message itself.

Will you intentionally put your school's beliefs about itself on display? At the World's Greatest High School, the first step is to recognize the beliefs that your school already has about itself and then to choose to take up the World's Greatest Values. Second, examine the way in which your school is already showcasing these beliefs, intentionally or unintentionally. Finally, craft a brand and start putting it on display. In later chapters, we're going to talk specifically about how to get your brand on display in your community and in your school in such a way as to make the biggest impact. In all, remember that your school's brand is not just about "images." Your brand is also the "gut feeling" that your school has about itself. The key, then, is to find out what this gut feeling is already, and then take up the values that will allow this sense to start shifting toward the World's Greatest High School brand.

Value #2: All students have futures.

At the World's Greatest High School, educators show off their belief that every student has a future and that educators have the ability to greatly impact that future.

Many of us act on feeling. Despite how advanced we are as human beings, our decision making, and our actions, and our way of living is still largely based upon the impulses that result from our gut checks (whether we know it or not). If you want to make people act, you can't just appeal to them on a cognitive, "heady" level - you have to get under their skin and into their hearts. Schools forget this when they post banners, posters, and plaques on the walls that communicate missions, ideas, and aspirations that don't connect to the hearts of those looking at them. That student in your class who sees the poster saying "Home of Champions" is not moved by the words; in fact, the student doesn't feel like a champion when the teacher tells them that they are "headed nowhere." Park talks a lot about "artwork on the wall" to point to the words at schools that are literally just wall-dressing. When a school puts out messages that it does *not* truly believe and act out, then they are just for show.

How, then, do you begin to create a brand that is connected to what the school believes? It all starts with "the why" of your school. Why does your school exist? In education today, there is an often-not-so-quiet war going on over this question. Rather than dialing into the larger dialogue happening in schools everywhere about this subject, engage in a conversation locally at your school about this. A format that we have found exceedingly successful is in grouping students, staff, parents, and community partners together at tables of four to six people. Place poster paper in front of them and ask them to silently begin drawing the symbols and words that they believe represent "why our school exists." After a few minutes, have one member from each group rotate to another group in the room and begin adding to the drawing that is waiting for them. Repeat this process. We are consistently amazed at what emerges from this exercise when people get out of the way of themselves and collectively, artistically put the purpose of the school on paper in this fashion. Two themes are always present: graduation and "futures." When your school discovers why it exists, it's now time to ask a vital question.

Does your school's brand (the outward expression of why it exists) belong to all, or just a select few? In most schools, the brand belongs to the Royal Family of the school. It speaks to their daily experience on campus and affirms their powerful position within it. What about your other students? Can all students relate to this brand? All staff? All parents? One school at which we have worked had a large banner over the entrance of the school that said, "Futures start here," alongside a giant graduation photo and a picture of the ACTUAL diploma students could receive through their hard work. Do you see how these branding images are all within reach of each person that looks upon it? Contrast this to another campus whose only branding on the side of the school was a giant color banner with a picture of the football team in action that read, "Our champions." When your branding concerns all who walk through your halls, it connects to the heart of things.

At the World's Greatest High School, the brand is the outward expression that this is a place where "I (a student) have a future." Will you provide your students with that kind of assurance and encouragement as they walk through your halls? It's as easy as placing the symbols of success in the corridors, in the classrooms, and within the curriculum. Begin by tapping into the collective wisdom of all those concerned with your school. Get them in a room and ask them why your school exists. Second, band with teachers to embed the symbols of success in everything that the school does. Finally, take every opportunity to remind students and reinforce the idea that ALL of them have a future. Next, let's talk about how teachers can assist in and be benefited by this process.

Value #3: No one gets anywhere without a teacher.

At the World's Greatest High School, educators recognize that no one gets anywhere without a teacher and that the impact of teachers is exponential. Without teachers, your school's product would not exist.

Who shakes the hands of students at your graduation ceremony? Is it the teachers who partnered daily with these students for the years past to achieve this honor? At many schools, we've often found it's the superintendent and the school board doing much of the handshaking. We fervently hold that people often inwardly feel what they are outwardly shown. At graduation, for example, as students are the center of the event, and when teachers are hand-in-hand alongside those students, the school community makes the inward connection between the educators whom worked with students each day and the great accomplishment that is symbolized by that diploma. Students don't just earn a piece of paper at the end of their one-and-a-quarter-decade journey through the public school system - the diploma is just a symbol of something larger! Similarly, the way in which we position teachers in the action, on the field, or on (or off) the stage is hugely important. How we position and treat teachers in the action shows your school's attitude toward those educators.

At graduation, should the photo of the student be displayed next to the photo of a teacher that the student named as their "most inspirational" alongside a picture of their family? At one graduation ceremony, each student named their most inspirational teacher and the name of this teacher was displayed on the jumbo-tron as the student walked down the red carpet. At another ceremony, a pre-arranged, pre-edited interview was played where each student in the graduating class talked about educators that had a significant impact upon them. At yet another ceremony, each teacher received an authentic, hand-written note from a student who considered them their most inspirational. In all these cases, the students and their accomplishment remained the focus, but teachers were showcased as key factors in the students' successes. Students remained the focus, while the teachers who partnered with them each day were also honored for their part.

At the World's Greatest High School, every opportunity is exhausted to place teachers alongside the symbolic successes of the school. From the football game - where players give their jerseys to their most inspirational teachers, to the Academic Rally - where students thank teachers publically for contributing to their success, the school knows the power of positioning teachers as respected, revered, appreciated, irreplaceable members of the school's family. If you want students to respect the school, the school must respect those who are within it. If you want the community to respect the school, showcase those that deserve the community's respect. When the outward symbols point to the amazing things happening inside the school, and when teachers are an integral part of what is being pointed to, the way in which the world sees your school transforms. Test this. Let us know if we are wrong.

Value #4: All students are gifted and talented.

At the World's Greatest High School, educators seek out and celebrate the gifts, talents, and skills that each person brings into the school. All gifts and talents are part of the brand.

Similar to the above point, the way that we showcase student success via our branding symbols is also vitally important. Is one symbol of success favored over others? Does the image of a football helmet have more emotional weight than the cap and gown at your school? Do the symbols sit well together or interact with one another? One school that we visited, for example, had two different logos used for the school - one used by the football team, and the other used by everyone else. There was a whole separate identity built around football that had little to do with the rest of the school's program. Likewise, at another school, the school's logo was synonymous with "football" at that school. When you asked the average person what the school's logo meant, the average person would say, "That means *Such-in-Such* Football." So the symbols that we utilize to showcase different types of student success are an important area of focus for your school.

First, it's important to have lots of different types of successes being shown through your branding. Reflect on how this may play out in your school. Does one program on campus have amazing looking t-shirts, while the others do not? Does the champion football team have a case of honor in the front office filled with trophies, while the champion band has its awards hidden in some back office somewhere? These are all common scenarios that we see at many of the schools that we visit. We believe that when students only see a single or very narrow type of success (or a narrow set of successes) being showcased on campus, their internal feelings about "not fitting in" to one of those buckets of success impacts their work, their way of being on campus, and their overall demeanor. There are students on your campus who have amazing talents and *never* get recognized for them in a meaningful, purposeful, systematic way. One of the many inventories that we provide campuses is our branding inventory. We make a list of all the symbols of success on your campus. Then we start grouping them together. How many of them relate to athletics? Which ones? How many relate to academics? Which content areas? How many (if any) relate to other on-campus activities? This allows for us to identify whom your campus tends to favor in terms of successes. You might find that there is an entire group of students (hundreds of them if your school is large enough) that don't have any "niches" at all into which to fit. We believe that when you give kids the chance to fit into niches of success, they are better off in *all areas of their school life* than if they are not fitting in at all! Impacting these students is as easy as simply showcasing more types of success in a way that they can have or find a place too.

Second, think about how well do your various branding symbols sit together. Are they in conflict, like two neighboring, warring nation-states? One campus that stands out to us had the football team and the soccer team (both highly successful) sharing the same field. There were conflicts about practice times, about what logos could be placed where (because they both had different ones), and about what types of shoes could be used on the grass. On another campus, the English department had pretty much monopolized the branding for the academic program of the school, with an image of Shakespeare standing over a book "Jesus style," arms outstretched painted on the side of a building. Every other department on campus simply could not stand behind this symbol, but they lacked the organization to get together to make a change. At this school, there was football and English. One of the administrators there, pointing at the wall where both logos sat painted said, "You would not know looking at this wall that we have one of the most competitive math programs in the State." The solution to these kinds of woes is not difficult to grasp.

At the World's Greatest High School, people from the school community sit together and brainstorm what branding already exists on campus that points to various types of student success. Then they notice the patterns of what is ever-present and what is typically missing. In many schools, they see that football is all over the place - while everything else is not. What would it be like for your school to create masterful symbology like what is created by top Fortune 500 companies? What if the different types of success at your school could sit together on the same shelf, wall, pamphlet, or t-shirt in such a way that as many students as possible could feel "plugged into" something? All it takes is a little planning, some conversation, and consistent action.

Value #5: Everyday is an opportunity to become the World's Greatest Me.

At the World's Greatest High School, each person on campus seeks to become a better version of "me" than the day before – and its members work purposefully to develop each person's gifts, talents, and skills.

When Park began the first academic rallies at the World's Greatest High School, many people resisted the mash of imagery that was placed under the banner of a single event. Like many high schools, most of the staff and students were accustomed to "fall sports rallies" and "spring sports rallies." They had no idea what to do with the type of rally ("the Academic Rally") that celebrated all types of student success. At the academic rallies, there were students, staff, and parents receiving medallions made of gold, foil-wrapped chocolate to celebrate successes of all kinds. There were athletes from all over campus wearing their jerseys. Rather than featuring the "*top* top" students alone, the rally showcased the successes of students of all kinds. It did not feature just one educator who was "the most popular"; instead, it featured many educators who were the "most inspirational." At the World's

Greatest High School, Park set a bar for celebrating the gifts, talents, and skills of all in the Academic Rally - a trend that spread, without exaggeration, across the nation. Has this tradition spread to your school?

There are few events at your school, beyond rallies and graduation, where everyone is gathered in a single place at a single time. For thousands of years, people have been gathering together for rituals that marked special moments and transitions between seasons of life; these rituals celebrate, entertain, and inspire. Schools rarely take advantage of the full power of these events. Many settle for graduation being the *only* school-wide event that celebrates academic success. If other celebrations of academic success are found at these schools, they often showcase a very narrow vision of what success looks like (e.g. perfect attendance, straight A's, honor role, etc.). When the school limits the ways in which success is showcased, it limits the ways in which students can find places in which to fit within the school. You have the chance to create something that touches the core of your students, staff, parents, and community members at the very core of what makes them human. All you have to do is create "diving board," "look at me" moments for people using the images of success at your school.

Have you ever climbed the high diving board above a pool? Have you ever experienced the moment of stepping to the edge and looking to see who is watching you? Nearly anyone who is a human being has had a moment such as this – a powerful, handful of seconds that sticks in our minds forever. Creating these moments for your school community only involves placing the various types of successes under one roof, under one event. The Academic Rally, for example, is a place where you can use the various branding at your school to show that "this is the place where people get to become the World's Greatest versions of themselves." Rather than having one student of the month, have as many as the staff can nominate. Instead of having a most popular teacher of the year, have most inspirational teachers named each month. Don't leave the thankless task of parenting without a "thank you"; instead, invite inspirational parents to the center of the rally and have them walk through the tunnel like champion athletes. Dress everyone in the symbols of success for your school – from jerseys, to uniforms, to medals, to the colors of their house or class. At the first Academic Rally, Park had all staff and students dressed in caps and gowns, as if graduation was about to begin. At the World's Greatest High School, the way in which the symbols of success are showcased is not by accident - and it's one of the most potent ways by which you can illustrate and reinforce how each person walking through your hallways is becoming a better person than they were the day before.

Value #6: Everything we do, we do with PRIDE.

At the World's Greatest High School, the school's one-of-a-kind culture of "Greatness" is clear in everything it does through its branding.

What makes your high school's brand distinct from others in your community or in your State? It's no accident that the best high schools have the most distinctive branding identities in their surrounding area. High schools can be like buzz-zones of pride, especially when the branding of the school is attuned to its one-of-a-kind culture. There is a high school in Orange County, California that has tuned its idea of "pride" to the way in which the school community cares for the school. All over campus, there is evidence that there are many hands at work in keeping the school clean, orderly, and beautiful (and it's not just the grounds crew doing this). There are plaques that sit in front of a dozen small gardens which state, "supported by *such-in-such*" business. There are marked parking spots next to the football field that say, "reserved for the *Joe Schmoe* Family, *blah blah* Football Pride." The graduation that this school holds embodies the "dignified graduation," where the unique student successes at that school are showcased. The valedictorian and salutatorian are joined on stage by a small group of "most inspirational" students who overcame significant hardship to stand there with a diploma in hand. Notice, that these are not canned, duplicated expressions of the school's individualism - each is a statement about what makes this school, and the community connected to it, absolutely one-of-a-kind.

When we are talking about "branding," we are not solely talking about the pictures that people think of when it comes to your school. We don't want you to be the world's next most recognizable fast-food chain! Instead, we are saying that your school has such greatness within it, such a uniqueness to it, that this is worth expressing in an organized, exceptional way. At the World's Greatest High School, the branding that is connected to it (the feelings, names, symbols, and slogans) speaks to the overall tapestry of *greatness* that is found therein. All that it takes to create this is to sit down with the exceptional people within your school - those that represent each group within, and have conversations about what branding is already being used, and how the school can work together to promote each school community member's favorite cause. You will always have interest groups within your school that will advocate for their favorite thing; instead of fighting this, embrace it and learn how you can advocate for each other.

In the end, ironically, what is required to have your school express its "pride" in this way is for the various advocates within the school to put down their personal pride enough to have this kind of conversation. These types of expressions in the way we are discussing simply will not happen on their own. Park often speaks of how his own Mentors and coaches were able to gather together the most mixed up bunch of people and form a team. Without such a coach, such a Mentor, or such a person such as you, the transformation about which we are speaking simply will not come to pass. As you read this, we hope that you will take license to *go and start these conversations*. We give you permission to do so! In fact, we strongly urge you and bless you to go out today and meet with the various people on your campus that represent each group and say, "I have an idea of how we can double our programs' successes this year. Would you be willing to sit down with me and a few other people for an hour to talk about that?" Though they might not be as excited as you are initially, through your caring heart and earnest authenticity, they will probably come around. Do you have the courage to take this step?

Summary

The feelings, names, symbols, and slogans of your school reflect what is happening within your campus. People outside look at your school and partake in this branding as a way of categorizing your school in their minds. Those inside your school hold the feelings; are swayed by the names, symbols, and slogans; and, consequently, can feel the pull of the disagreements between these different "brandings" when they are not getting along. At the World's Greatest High School, courageous individuals band together to shape the branding in such a way that it expresses the unified, true nature of the school within. Together, the school community uses the branding in a strategic way to communicate to the outside world and to its members about what is happening within the school. In the next chapter, we'll discuss how we can strategically employ your brand to do wonders for your campus.

Blueprint Questions:

1. Thinking about the definition we presented at the start of this chapter, what branding already exists at your school? Make a list.
2. To what "interest" or "faction" does each feeling, name, symbol, and slogan belong?
3. Do these belong to the whole school, or just one group?
4. Who are the key persons attached to each of these?
5. What does each piece of branding communicate to the community about your school?
6. What does each piece of branding indicate you value as a school?

Dares:

1. Have groups of students answer the questions above using pictures on poster paper.
2. Gather the various key persons together. Ask them how *you* can better assist them in communicating the greatness of their programs.

World's Greatest Marketing

Chapter 9

"Marketing your school is not about getting its logo out there: it's about marketing the futures of your students."

If "branding" is the gut feelings, names, symbols, and slogans used to identify your school's educational program, "marketing" is the strategies by which this brand is communicated. The brand is the "what is being said," while marketing is "how it is being said." In the previous chapter, we gave you a lot to think about in terms of what your brand says about the product that your school produces - graduates. In this chapter, we are going to talk about how to communicate your brand in such a way that is consistent with the World's Greatest Values. Chances are, there is much mixed messaging happening at your school already - so much, in fact, that there is no clear sense of how your school has collectively decided to get the word out there about who your students, staff, and parents are as well as what you hope to accomplish together.

Let's take a brief look at some of the mixed messaging systems that are already in place on your campus. Do you have a front office at your school with posters or plaques displaying the mission statement of the school? Take a moment to go there and write down the mission, vision, or purpose statements that are displayed. While you're there, does your district have a mission, vision, or purpose statement also displayed nearby? Jot those down too. On your way back to your office or classroom, does the school have a motto inscribed on a building anywhere on campus - perhaps on a marque at the front of the school? What does that motto state about your school? While in your office or classroom, dig up an old memo or school letter, and then take a look at the letterhead. Is there a motto or inscription there? Writing all these down next to one another, are these all the same message? Just wait! Do you have "expected schoolwide learning results" (ESLRs) or learning goals posters on campus? What do these say? In your experience, do you see any differences between these various message systems on campus? Do you notice that they are all saying quite different things?

In contrast, if you walk onto one of the campuses we have visited, you'll see the word "dreamers" plastered on every memo and letter sent by the school. Yet the first word that you'll see on nearly every poster inside classrooms, which describes their students as part of their school-wide learning goals is - no joke, "practical." Similarly, if you came to any campus event, you would also see different messages being sent about "who we are" depending on what event you attended. So many messages are being sent in so many varied ways that the words lose their meaning - and mission statements just become more artwork on the wall.

What would happen if we harnessed the collective energy of the same message being sent out in consistent ways? This chapter will shed much light on the answer to that question.

Value #1: We are what we believe - what we believe unifies us.

At the World's Greatest High School, we know that our beliefs greatly influence how your school goes about marketing its product.

As we delve into this value and how it relates to the marketing in which your school engages, remember that the product your school creates and sells is the educational experience students have and the future that educational experience creates (e.g. graduation, career, family, etc.). When your school is perfectly aligned in its beliefs about what your school's brand is all about and how to channel that brand through a pre-planned set of clear messages, your school can reach the World's Greatest potential that we are discussing here. However, when the school believes many different things about itself depending on what "camp" you walk into (e.g. football team, band, the hallway in front of your classroom, the Social Studies Department, the administration, the PTA), and thus the messaging is different and, perhaps, conflicting, the school's brand is muddied and often completely unflattering of the school. Without a single brand and without a set of core, pre-planned marketing strategies, your school's messaging can actually harm you and prevent you and your school from getting what it actually wants.

At the World's Greatest High School, Park had the benefit of opening the school in such a way that allowed the entire staff to be on the same page about the school's brand and the ways in which the school would go about marketing this brand. One of the ways that Park and his staff decided to market and teach this "World's Greatest High School" brand was by holding an opening rally with students the first day of school. During this rally, the staff was the first to model the school's cheer. In fact, the staff was so bold in yelling that they out-performed hundreds of students in this chant. From the start, the staff sent the message to the students that this was the best place around to go to school. Here, the staff were excited about being part of the action - not hiding in their classrooms during the rally or sitting silently in the reserved staff chairs. In short, Park and his staff believed in having a core strategy to get out their beliefs about being the World's Greatest High School. They believed this was important and this belief drove them to market and teach their brand in this unified way.

Many schools make the mistake of "doing marketing" in the wrong order. First, these mistaken schools decide on the type of marketing strategies they will use. Second, they assume that these strategies themselves will start creating a brand for the school. Each of these schools fail to realize that they *already* have a brand - one that is based in the beliefs that the school holds about itself and the values that it lives out each day. Each of these schools also fail to realize that the beliefs that the school holds, shape and limit the kind of marketing in which the school engages. At the World's Greatest High School, the first step in marketing is not creating a "community-parent liaison" to start crafting marketing strategies for the school or opening a Facebook or Twitter account. Instead, it's vital to start by figuring out what the school already stands for – and the mixed messages that various groups are already sending about the school from camp to camp. Then we can go back to the previous chapters and take steps to infuse the World's Greatest Values into your day-to-day work as a school. Only this will truly impact the school brand in the way we are describing here. Finally, and only then, start thinking about the messaging systems that your school will utilize to communicate this brand out into the world. Start thinking about how the beliefs you hold as a campus impact the ways that you go about creating these marketing strategies. Who's going to be receiving most of these messages? What information channels (online and offline) are worth using? How can you centralize or coordinate the ways that these messages about your school go out? How do your answers to these questions reveal the beliefs that you have at your school regarding marketing your school brand? This chapter is dedicated to answering many of these questions by looking at how you can market in a way that honors each of the World's Greatest Values.

Value #2: All students have futures.

At the World's Greatest High School, educators know that every student has a future and that educators have the ability to market that future as a strategy for improving student success.

When Park was leading the World's Greatest High School, they had a tradition at rallies called "Stand Up for Achievement." This tradition involved an announcer reading a list of the great things that were happening on campus. Rather than having a small team or an individual walk through the smoking tunnel with strobe lights flashing, the master of ceremonies would read out the names of students, teams, groups, clubs, teachers, departments, etc. and these groups would stand together and remain standing until everyone was recognized. More than three quarters of the room would be standing at the rally at the same time, being recognized for the great things that they were doing. The message that this sent was simple: "There are *already* amazing things happening on our campus. Look how many people are doing such great things! This is the kind of school where I can be part of a group of people doing great things!" Where most schools have a tradition of selectively recognizing the top one-to-ten percent of students and staff, the World's Greatest High School fine-tunes its marketing system in such a way that many people are "caught up" in the mix. This is not about giving everyone a trophy or award. This is about showing the great amount of success already at your school.

For your marketing to be the most effective on your campus, it has to appeal to the most people. When your messages are microscopically focused, the pay-off is also microscopic. One kid might feel fantastic for a few days about receiving that one certificate, but when you expand the focus to recognize a multitude of greatness at your school, more people can be "feeling fantastic" together. Perhaps you have experienced attending an amazing event by yourself. When you try to communicate with others how amazing the event was, you can't quite capture the feeling and communicate it. However, go to that same event with a group of friends, and you'll be able to talk about that feeling and re-experience it for a lifetime. At the World's Greatest High School, marketing is the way by which students can collectively experience that feeling of "we're going somewhere" together. All you have to do is craft group experiences to make this possible. Further, by making this brand of recognition ongoing, you can reinforce the gains experienced by all.

The first step is not that you get a meeting started to talk about the school's marketing; Instead, the first step is expanding your own vision - refining your own eye's ability to see the amazing constellation of sweetness that exists on your campus today. If you cannot see it, how will others? In a way, you have to transplant your ability to see all the "great things happening" upon others in your staff, at your PTA meeting, or anywhere where people are looking at student success. We have often been so hypnotized by the focus upon *lack* of results that we ignore the pile of evidence of amazing "turn-arounds," family transformations, and claiming of future generations of prosperity by the multitude of students passing through your halls. Once you have a grasp upon the ability to see the broad array of good at your school, then you are ready to get together with other educators and begin talking about how we can expand our celebrations to include all, rather than the accomplishments of the top one-percent or ten-percent of your school.

Value #3: No one gets anywhere without a teacher.

At the World's Greatest High School, educators market that no one gets anywhere without a teacher and that the impact of teachers is exponential.

We know an educator who watched one of his students get drafted into one of the most recognized college football teams in the United States. The school had so grasped onto the idea of marketing the future of this student and how teachers helped him get there, they decided to hold a formal signing ceremony at the school, where the press could be present and see how the school was part of this student's path toward this amazing success. What caught our attention was that the student invited his most inspirational teacher to stand behind him and his parents as he signed a mock-contract, symbolizing his choice to "sign" for this college. One of the greatest marketing strategies that the World's Greatest High School employs is giving teachers "a seat at the table" when it comes to marketing the success of students.

As the quote that leads this chapter states, marketing your school is not about getting its logo out there; it's about marketing the futures of your students. An even more powerful strategy is when this focus upon "futures" is coupled with recognition of those who made the future possible. Since no one gets anywhere without a teacher, the school community makes a point of always showing educators alongside the various student successes on campus. At celebrations, rather than simply handing a student an award for their accomplishment, a number of things happen. First, the press is called, because they are one of the many local pipelines to the outside world to show the great things that are happening for students. Second, names are read ceremoniously and the award is handed to the student by his or her most inspirational teacher. Finally, the moment is captured on video, via photo, and placed on social networks, in the yearbook, and on the school's website.

In the current western tradition, there is an emphasis placed upon lone personal achievement. We love stories how an individual "picked themselves up by their own bootstraps" and made it across the metaphorical finish line. This tradition is alive and well in schools and poses a significant roadblock to marketing futures at your school. When a student sees an older peer seemingly crossing the finish line alone, the most they can say is, "Wow, I hope I can do that." Conversely, when a student sees an older peer walking arm-in-arm with an inspirational educator, coach, or mentor to the finish, that student says, "Hey, I have that teacher! Maybe she can help me too!" Accordingly, one of the first obstacles that you must overcome as a school is the long-standing, ever-entrenched position of honoring individuals alone. Instead, we want to honor the collective greatness that is achieved together. If you are reading this and you disagree, we imagine that you greatly value your own individual achievement; yes, you have done amazing things, but was there not a single person that helped you along the way? Would it not represent the World's Greatest You to allow others to be recognized for their part of your success?

Value #4: All students are gifted and talented.

At the World's Greatest High School, educators seek out and publically celebrate (or market) the gifts, talents, and skills that each person brings into the school.

Marketing the futures of all students is far more effective than marketing the success of one. For nearly a century (at least in the history of the contemporary secondary school in the United States), the tradition has largely been to celebrate the Royal Family of the school alone. When the majority of students see the same few students paraded to the front of the auditorium or gym time and time again, and they don't see anyone like themselves in the mix, then there is little motivation derived from this celebration. How can most students with a "D" average be motivated by seeing the same straight-'A' students celebrated for the tenth time? How can a student with poor attendance be motivated by the one student who has perfect attendance? This simply does not add up, because the gap is too wide for many to find their way across on their own. At the World's Greatest High School, a new tradition is created of expanding our vision of student success and getting those successes in front of as many eyes as possible. What would happen at your school if every student felt like they could relate to another person's success on campus? What if they could relate to the successes of dozens of others? Could it be that they might join in on the success if such opportunities existed and such opportunities were marketed to them daily?

Schools also have a reputation in their communities. Some schools carry a "No Hope High School" or "Mediocre High" reputation, in part because not enough types of success have been effectively marketed by the school. Instead, we want to place in front of your community so many mentions of the amazing "futures" that students are creating, such that your community can see to what degree "amazing" is the average product of your school. Just as your vocabulary as a school must expand to include more types of success, the community around you also has to be trained to understand that success is not just "honor roll." There is so much success already on your campus that you cannot keep track of it all. All you have to do is capture a large enough subsection of that success and start conversing with the community about it.

This type of conversation with the community, which expands the definition of success celebrated by your school, does not start by sending out "blasts," newsletters, or creating a new school brochure. Instead, it starts by talking with the students on your campus about the successes that they have experienced, how they became successful, and getting that information out to the other students at your school. When Park was at the World's Greatest High School, this was done by simply bringing the whole champion soccer team to the stage with their championship banner and having them thank those who had an impact upon them during the school year. Those few minutes of these students saying thank you to various educators and coaches on campus sent the following message to other students: "This teacher that I runs my second period class is respected by some of our school's best athletes; maybe I can respect him or her too." Simultaneously, celebrated students are provided their inspiring "diving board" moments of being up front with eyes on them together. This team of students, and all students on campus, get to partake in their experience of being celebrated for their success. For you, incidents such as these become "marketable moments" of futures being crafted before the eyes of the school community. All you have to do is capture them in film and photo and get them out to as many eyes as possible.

Value #5: Everyday is an opportunity to become the World's Greatest Me.

At the World's Greatest High School, each person on campus seeks to become a better version of "me" than the day before – and its members work purposefully to develop each person's gifts, talents, and skills. That journey of progress is marketed to all.

Though we emphasize the accomplishment of large groups of people, including students, staff, parents, and other community members and partners, personal growth also enters into the mix. Here's the key aspect, though, that most schools miss: Personal growth is best celebrated when others can relate to the journey taken – not the final accomplishment. Students at your school might not be able to relate to one's desire to enter the Air Force, but they can relate to the trials and tribulations that he or she had to fight through to get there – problems at home, difficulty with finances, struggling to pass classes. It's just like in a movie: two minutes of the film is the "happily ever after," but the other two hours are about the struggle to get there. We *love* stories of struggle that lead to triumph. You have to tell the story of the struggle.

There are many stories that are "archetypal" - that is, stories that any person in any culture can relate to. These include, (1) rags to riches, (2) failure to fame, (3) nobody became a somebody, (4) overcoming giants, and many others. When you discover that a student, staff member, or community member has embodied one of these types of stories through their lived experiences, this is an opportunity for you to market that story and that struggle toward a future. Tell the story of transformation. At a rally at one school in Southern California, Park witnessed the podium being given to the coach of the debate team; he began giving a fiery speech about how his debate team had been winning the competition locally. Before that moment, few people on campus even knew that such a team existed at the school - but now, as the debate team stood in the wings watching their coach, the multitude of students at the school got to witness a piece of the struggle of this rag-tag team of debate kids. The seeds of a story of success were being planted. For these students on this debate team, they had renewed motivation to be better versions of themselves because now the school was looking to them in expectation of victory. In the hallways, students wished the debate team members "good luck," and said, "kick that rival school's [butt]!" All it took was a podium moment such as this to plant those seeds.

At the World's Greatest High School, we strategize to give these kinds of podium moments to people on campus. These moments do many things. First, they provide a way by which to market the emerging futures coming into focus each day. Second, they provide motivation for students to become a version of themselves able to accomplish the success promised. Finally, when students see one another "in the struggle," they naturally want to join in and be part of the action – just like you fantasize about joining the action on the movie screen. It's critical to show the struggle, and give students their moments in the limelight, and market futures; reinforcing the expectation that these futures will come true with hard work and by developing one another.

Value #6: Everything we do, we do with PRIDE.

At the World's Greatest High School, the school's one-of-a-kind culture of "Greatness" is clearly marketed in everything it does.

Just as students have the opportunity to be showcased to the community inside and outside your school through their successes, the unique avenues of success within your school can likewise be celebrated and marketed. School cultures tend to emphasize what is not working well. We dedicate entire meetings to discussing what is not working and even draft hundred-page plans to address what is malfunctioning. Should not at least the same amount of energy, if not more, be dedicated to what is going well at your school? What kind of impact would we have if the focus was upon what was working over what was not? Many schools are taking this leap and are using the various marketing vehicles available to them as a means by which to start these conversations.

A great example is the t-shirts at your school. It's possible that your school does not have t-shirts at all, outside in physical education and the locker room. Similarly, what do the letterman jackets say about your school? Can only athletes obtain one? The apparel worn by your students is one of the most under-appreciated marketing methods on campus. They are not under-appreciated because schools don't have such apparel; instead, the problem is that most schools don't realize how much power they hold. For example, the letterman jacket has been a staple at high schools since the early twentieth century, but very few schools have fully teased out the power that these jackets hold. As you probably already know, these jackets are universal symbols of youth success in the United States. They are a place where the various achievements, typically athletic, are sewn on in patch form. At the World's Greatest High School, Park and the team of educators and coaches, decided that at their school, students could letter in almost anything. They had "Varsity English" students. They had "Varity Activities" students. Wherever a student was plugged into the one-of-a-kind facets of the school's program, a student could get recognized for it. This was one of the ways that the school decided to express its unique sense of marketing. You and your school must find what is precious and unique about your school and market that to the world at large and to those that are campus-connected. At the World's Greatest High School, you communicate your school's uniqueness on purpose everywhere you can.

First, consider if there are already traditions at your school that can be built upon as vehicles of communicating the school's unique sense of *pride*. Second, ask if the avenues of success within that tradition can be expanded to include more people and/or be better broadcast to those inside and outside the school. Finally, how can the various interest groups on campus band together to create a unified marketing strategy to communicate the school's brand?

Summary

While the school's branding revolves around "what is being said," the school's marketing is concerned with "how it is being said." Like any other aspect of the curriculum at your school, you must teach the brand. The way in which you teach that brand to the school and to the community that surrounds it is through your marketing. First, communicate how there are more successes happening on your campus than not. Second, place teachers alongside the various successes that are being marketed. Third, give those being celebrated well-thought-out, dignified podium moments that allow others to experience their struggle and relate to it. Finally, build unified strategies to communicate the school's brand to the world in a systematic, planned way. At the World's Greatest High School, just as you plan for the individual greatness of each member within, you have to create a marketing plan to support this.

We offer a school marketing strategy session via our website at www.worldsgreatesthighschool.com. Check it out!

Blueprint Questions:

1. Thinking of the last school celebration you attended, what successes were celebrated there?
2. What are the ways in which your school already teaches your school's brand to your students?
3. What is one school celebration that could be enhanced to provide more epic, podium moments to showcase stories of struggle and triumph?

Dares:

1. Access the school marketing strategy session at the website mentioned above.
2. Complete the marketing plan steps found therein.
3. Choose one school celebration to better this year and follow through.

World's Greatest You

Chapter 10

"It starts with you."

The number one question we get on our website and at our talks is, "Where do we start?" Chances are, after reading this far into *Building the World's Greatest High School*, you have many ideas about where you should start this journey. In our discussions with educators who have recently been taught the World's Greatest Values, we see a common thread of a great passion for making change happen for their schools. However, there's also the lingering question of, "Where do I begin? There's so much to be done!" We have been fortunate to have Mentors in our lives who have pointed us to the single best place to start any journey, any task, or any major undertaking as great as building a school like the one we have discussed in this volume. The place to start is within *you*.

During both of our first years as educators, we were really concerned with looking like good teachers and doing the things that good teachers do. You can probably relate to this in a huge way.

Our credential programs spend so much time evaluating us on "doing the right thing," that we forget about "being the right kind of person." However, if our teaching "looks good," but our hearts say "we don't believe that all students have futures," then our teaching is not the best it can be, because our heart is in the wrong place entirely. Similarly, much staff development is focused now upon learning how to teach with the best strategies. In reality, we know that even with the best teaching strategies, an educator who does not believe in his or her students is not the best for students. The focus needs to be on becoming the best "me" as both a human being and a teacher - from the core outward. It starts with what we believe, then moves to what we do privately, and lastly bleeds outward into who we are in the classroom and for our school community at large.

Plainly: The first step in Building the World's Greatest High School is to begin building a better you from the foundation up. This chapter will start you in this process, but it's only a beginning. What you'll see by the end of this chapter is that the process of becoming the World's Greatest Me is a lifelong one. This journey begins with the World's Greatest Values that we believe and attempt to live out each day.

Value #1: We are what we believe – what we believe unifies us.

Or, more appropriately: At the World's Greatest High School, your beliefs shape you.

Throughout this book, we have given you a lot to think about in terms of how our collective beliefs at the World's Greatest High School can impact our school, our students, and our community. What about ourselves? How can what I personally believe as an educator impact what I do in the classroom? This entire chapter is dedicated to this topic. First, however, let's talk about what is necessary to begin the journey of being the World's Greatest Me: It takes an out-of-body experience.

Park had one of his first out-of-body experiences during his first years teaching. He describes the incident: "Before I started thinking about becoming the World's Greatest Me, I had doubts about who I was as a teacher and if I was going to be successful. When I was with my students, I was very mechanical – following the lesson plans in the textbook to the letter. If you have ever taught middle school, you can imagine what my first year as a teacher was like, especially as I was going through this identity crisis. It was chaos. During my first formal observation, I went to my friend Jim and asked for an experiment that would impress the principal. He said he would take care of the whole thing, prepare it for me, and leave it in my classroom. The day of the observation, the principal walked in and started writing on the clipboard right away. I was sweating bullets, thinking 'unless this is a dynamite lesson, I'm going to lose my job.' First, I covered the safety procedures. 'You never put your thumb over the test tube and shake it,' I firmly told my students. Second, I put the purple cabbage juice in the test tube and placed a drop of lemon juice, and waited for the magic to happen as the color would change. In disbelief, I realized that there was no change. I saw the principal writing faster. I poured a whole lot of lemon juice in and still nothing happened! Then, I put ammonia in. 'Ok watch the change.' Still, no change! Right at that panicked moment, I put my thumb over the top of that test tube and began to shake it. In front of the principal and all my students, I burnt my thumb! At that moment, one kid raised his hand and asked, 'What are you trying to teach us?' The principal walked up smiling with a note asking 'Could it not be cabbage juice?' My friend Jim had played a complete prank on me. That got me thinking a lot about how people see me from the outside." It took an experience such as this for Park to see how others were seeing. This showed Park a side of him he had not seen - one that was not the kind of teacher he wanted to be.

To begin the process of becoming the World's Greatest Me, one has to step outside oneself and begin thinking about what he or she believes based upon how one is living their life. Do I believe in the World's Greatest Values? How do each of these values show up in my life as I teach? One of the first things that Park did to start this journey was to seek out Mentors who could reflect back to him how he was "showing up" in the world. Just as his friend, Jim, gave him the opportunity to experience how mechanical Park was being in the classroom, friendships and mentorships could provide you with one of the most poignant mirrors you could experience in your lifetime. Park's evaluation went fine, by the way. He kept his job.

As you go through this chapter, think about how the World's Greatest High School is a place for you to develop as a human being, just as it is a place for each student and staff member to be the World's Greatest Me each day. It is a place where you too can become the best version of yourself to date. It starts with what you believe and translates into how you carry yourself into your work with your students, peers, and community. Let's look through the rest of the World's Greatest Values to illustrate this.

Value #2: All students have futures.

At the World's Greatest High School, educators know that every student has a future and that educators views about student success greatly impacts that future.

Much of this book has laid a significant case toward this fact - that all students have futures. However, when we are discussing *you* becoming the World's Greatest Me, a key question regarding student futures is, "What kind of future do you anticipate for your students?" Imagine taking a glass of water and adding a drop of red dye. How much water would have to flow through that cup to remove the scarlet hue we have added? Similarly, when students come into our classrooms, we often regard them as crystal clear cups until we place a drop of dye for each infraction, sin, or irritation (whatever word you choose). Then, the process of cleansing begins - or the water gets more and more red with each infraction. This is the way that many educators approach their work with students and their beliefs about the students' futures: "If the students show me enough hard work, commitment, and good behavior, then I'll believe that 'great' things await them." We are presenting in this book, an alternative view to this way of looking at students.

You have complete control in seeing your students as having futures. Imagine that same glass of crystal clear water, but with some oil added instead of dye. If you have seen this before, you know that the water and oil will remain separate. Regardless of how much oil you add, the water within that glass will remain as clear as the day it was placed there. What if your students were like this glass of water and oil? What if, regardless of the amount of oil within the glass, you could look at them (and that crystal clear water) and say, "I can still see the good in you. There is much work to be done, but we can make this well"? Here's the mind-bending part though: You're the one adding the oil - not the student. You can choose to add a drop, a gallon, or none at all. From the moment a student walks through your door to the moment that they exit for the final time, you have complete control of how you view your students - independent of their actions, behaviors, and ability to convince you that they are undeserving. You are in complete control. You can choose to focus upon the oil or the water - the negative or the innate qualities of goodness within each student.

Thus far in my teaching career, Brandon has been one of my most challenging students. Every day, it felt almost like destiny that we would be butting heads within the first five minutes of class. It was torture for both of us. I'll never forget one day when a breaking point was reached. I stepped outside my classroom door to "counsel him" about his behavior, saying, "Brandon, I can tell you don't like me at all. What if your performance in my class and your like for me were not related?" Brandon smiled back at me and said, "Dr. White, what if your idea of my 'performance' and your like for me was *completely* related?" In that moment, I was pretty furious at what Brandon said to me. However, he was completely right. My view of him was entirely tarnished by weeks of conflict. Even if he did a good deed, my mind was caught up in the habitual pattern of reacting to him and reinforcing my polluted view of his prospects in my classroom.

To become the World's Greatest Me, we all have to become aware of our habitual patterns toward our students - individually and collectively. We have a groove that we have reinforced over our entire teaching career. To attempt to step out of our habitual patterns means that we will have to butt heads with our own stubborn reactions and biases. Some teachers will fool themselves into easily saying, "every student is appreciated in my class," but will refuse to look at how the unseen patterns of their hearts impact student performance. How is your view of students' futures impacting your late work policy, the restrictions you place on students making up exams, or in the way you keep your classroom managed and orderly? Could it be that you already anticipate your students' futures based upon old habits of what success looks like to you? What happens when a student operates outside this roadmap of success? The first step is to notice where we are triggered - to pay special attention to when our anger or frustration arises. We believe that students can be our greatest teachers of how we need to grow - precisely where they push our buttons most. Will you be willing to see your students with clear eyes?

Value #3: No one gets anywhere without a teacher.

At the World's Greatest High School, educators recognize that no one gets anywhere without a teacher and that the impact of teachers is exponential. Teachers maximize their ability to build the perfect, customized learning experiences for each student and his or her specific capacities.

The role of a teacher is to place his or her students in an uncomfortable learning situation where success is questionable - and then assist students toward success by playing upon their strengths and capacities in development. When I first started practicing the martial arts, I was not accustomed to having a teacher of this kind. He knew me so well and he made it his mission to push me in just the right way - to the point just before breaking and then having me hang out in that place of uncertainty where the real growth could happen. One of the "worst" days in my memory, I walked into class and he said, "Do 200 push ups; take as long as you need." I struggled through twenty-five, seventy-five, 125, and finally 200 push-ups. It took me nearly one hour to do it. Had it been a single more push-up, I think I would have walked out. However, he knew me so well that he hand-chose the exact number that would take me to the breaking point and give me success right there on the edge. Could you provide such an experience for students? This is not about creating breaking points - it's about knowing your students' edges.

To teach at the level of the World's Greatest Me, it requires that you know your students to such a degree that you know their individual strengths, weaknesses, and capacities. So much of education focuses upon groups of students in the classroom. The edu-sphere asks, "Who are your English Language Learners?" "Who are your Learning Disabled students?" "Who has accommodations in their IEP?" Along with these questions, the World's Greatest High School asks, "What capacity is Katarina developing this week?" This is a major shift that requires much from us as educators. Stepping into this level of familiarity with out students requires that we take a vulnerable position - as someone having intimate knowledge about each individual student and becoming an advocate on their behalf. The distance that the gradebook affords us is gone because we are vying for the success of our students on a personal level. Their success is our celebration. Their success is something in which we are personally invested. Their failure can harm us or let us down.

To become the World's Greatest Me, we have to be willing to place ourselves in the vulnerable position of advocating for individual students and fully owning our impact upon them, or lack thereof. We have to place our heart into the act of teaching in such a way that failure creates a sting. This requires an openness of heart that is hard for many of us, as we have to be open to the letdowns and the consequences of being personally invested. Consider, though, how our students regard us when we move from public school teacher to "your teacher," "your mentor," or "your advocate." What will be made possible in their eyes, knowing that someone with the strength such as you - one who has enjoyed so much success in your life - has stepped behind them in support? Could you make such a commitment to a student? A greater you may be required to take up such a mantle of responsibility.

Value #4: All students are gifted and talented.

At the World's Greatest High School, educators cultivate the gifts, talents, and skills that each person brings into the school.

Just as we must know the individual capacities of our students, including their strengths and weaknesses, the World's Greatest You have the ability as an educator to sense into the strengths of students and tease out the gems that could be considered their gifts and talents. So many teachers throughout the world are solely laser-focused upon their individual content areas. One teacher might say, "I teach English Literature," and never look at a student's capacities outside this narrow realm. We hold the attitude that teachers are guides to developing students through the lens of their course subjects. They are building a literacy that will enrich the whole life of the student. For example, one of us might say, "We develop students *through* the focus of English Literature." That is, though we primarily work with the subject-matter of poems and essays, we are really developing each student to their ultimate capacities, especially in those areas in which they are gifted and talented. Therefore, what is asked of us, as the World's Greatest Me, is to be watchful of those unique aspects of each of our students which could be considered their personal gifts and talents. We can use the literacies we teach to impact the whole student and his or her gifts, talents, and skills.

You also have unique gifts and talents that deserve your focus. You also are on a path of development as a human being and as an educator. Are you able to name the individual gifts and talents that you bring uniquely into the classroom? How do you utilize these to better the learning experiences of your students? To better your school at large? As a culture of educators, we're obsessed with the extremes offered by focusing upon how we teach (pedagogy) and what we teach (content). We often ignore what brought us into the classroom in the first place - some calling or talent that needed to be acknowledged by taking on one of the most singularly challenging and distinctive careers in the world. The next step for you, as with your students, is to develop these gifts and talents each day.

Value #5: Everyday is an opportunity to become the World's Greatest Me.

At the World's Greatest High School, each person on campus seeks to become a better version of "me" than the day before - and its members work purposefully to develop each person's gifts, talents, and skills.

People need personal trainers who know the areas in which they are being developed and can hold their feet to the fire when accountability is needed. Both you and your students need a personal trainer (Mentor or advocate) to assist you in developing your individual gifts and talents. You can be the personal trainer, of sorts, for your students as they develop their gifts and talents. Just as we have discussed throughout this text, becoming an advocate for students requires you to become deeply knowledgeable with their strengths and needs and to assist them in developing toward success. We may have neglected to mention, however, the transformation that may be required of you to do this kind of work. Do you know the names of all the students within your classes? Do you know what individual skills each is developing right now? Do you know their individual goals for the future and how you can help them get there? Few educators, including us, can answer "yes" to all these questions. This illustrates the constant pull we can feel as educators to become more invested and more in-the-know about our students and their individual capabilities, goals, and dreams. Each day, could you learn one more student's name than the day before. If you spoke to two students per class per day about their individual interests, could you be more able to serve them then the day before? Could you make a point of attending two to four student events this year and simply socialize with your students and be a greater part of the school community in this respect? Would you be willing to make it a point to utilize the interests of your students as springboards for activities in your classroom?

Just as you can be this kind of advocate for your students, you need an advocate of your own – a Mentor who can assist you in developing. An entire chapter of this book was dedicated to the need for this kind of a person in our lives. Currently, there are few formal systems within the school that encourage this kind of partnership. Even where formal mentorships are provided, they often do not reach the level of "Mentor" (capital M) about which we are speaking. Mentors are rarely found by asking someone, "Hi! Will you be my mentor?" Instead, Mentorship is developed over time through long-standing relationships and the "eagleship" (to quote one of our Mentors) of a great person who decides to bless us with his or her presence in our lives. There is a whole cadre of "coaches" for hire out in the world as a way by which to develop one's capacities. While these coaches are a huge part of my development, and I recommend professional coaching to anyone, one need not always seek out a professional to develop in the way that we are suggesting here. Simply spending time with great people (especially educators) wherever you find them will assist in your growth. Develop a relationship with them and talk with them about teaching. By building relationships with these kinds of people, you can grow in the places in which you need the most development.

Value #6: Everything we do, we do with PRIDE.

At the World's Greatest High School, the school's one-of-a-kind culture of "Greatness" is clear in everything it does.

With the release of numerous recent films about education, an ever-increasing focus has been placed upon the way in which educators are developed throughout the United States. As a norm, teachers have little say in the way that they are developed as professionals from the moment they leave a teacher credential program to their last day of teaching. If the school is paying for it, the school or the school district is probably deciding when and where an educator is being developed. While we were grateful for much of the learning opportunities afforded to us inside the system, both Park and I began looking outside district-mandated professional development to develop as human beings. To become my World's Greatest Me, I had to travel half way around the world, learn to meditate, earn a doctorate, and a two-year coaching certification. For Park, he had to do much more over many decades. Thus, just as your school has a one-of-a-kind culture to express, you have a unique path in your development that you must follow.

What interests you? To become the World's Greatest version of yourself, what things do you want to have, be, and do in your life that you have yet to undertake? Do you want to learn certain skills, take certain classes, or have certain experiences? Do you want to travel? Do you want to return to school or find a whole new school?

Similarly, what have you been avoiding? Is there something you have been working *not* to do? The answers to these questions provide some clues about what the World's Greatest You should do. Is there something that you have been wanting to do, but you have been shying away from it because of the time commitment or the work involved? If you had just one life, one chance, would you take it and go for it?

Who are your role models? More appropriately: Why are these people your role models? What qualities within these people attract you to them? What aspects of their lives do you want to make alive in your own life?

How much happier would we be if we spent more time developing ourselves in the areas we need to develop, rather than stomaching the hours of time wasted in pursuits that are outside our needs? Can you imagine taking those hundreds of hours of meetings and trainings that you did not truly need and spending them on development in the areas in which you (or your Mentors) know would benefit you? What would happen if you and your Mentor-advocates began directing your professional development as an educator and began working daily toward becoming the World's Greatest You each day?

Summary

Becoming the World's Greatest You requires that you expand your vision. First, expand your vision to see yourself as an educator in development and begin to see what others see in you. Second, expand your vision of your students and their successes, allowing students to show you more of what they have to offer as human beings. Third, begin developing your students in their unique capacities, taking note of your individual students' needs instead of focusing upon them as a group of students. Finally, begin your journey of developing yourself as a human being. A happier, more wholly developed you will not only be a better, happier teacher, but a better, happier human being as well.

Blueprint Questions:

1. What do you want to have in your life as a whole?
2. What do you want to do in your life?
3. Who and/or what do you want to be?
4. What legacy would you like to leave when you retire from teaching?

Dares:

1. Spend at least three minutes per class period getting to know one or two of your students better as individuals.
2. Personally select and attend a training of your choosing, whether or not it's directly related to education.

3. Find and spend time with a Mentor. Meet regularly with them throughout the month.

Celebrating the World's Greatest

Chapter 11

How to take this to the next level.

We are ecstatic that you are gazing upon this page. We have come such a long way to arrive at this moment. As a culture of educators, much happened in the past that has led to this moment in our history. If you have not had your head buried under a rock the past few years, you know that much is being questioned about the purpose of schools, how teachers teach, and the ways in which students are performing (and not) in classrooms today. We can whole-heartedly say that the ways in which the world at large is attempting to meet these challenges will only find mediocre success. If truly the goal of the school is to guarantee the success of all those who walk through its halls, what is being offered by the edu-sphere today simply won't do - because the whole of what is required is not being addressed.

What is being asked of us as educators is nothing short of a miracle. We are feeling the pressures to make school relevant and possible for everyone. Students, parents, the administration, and the community are demanding from us more than they have ever asked before. Everyone is so busy asking the wrong questions. This provides you, the individual teacher reading this right now, an opportunity that may never come again. While everyone is distracted, you can make the individual changes that you know will have an amazing impact upon your school community. With all the pressure being placed upon teachers to do specific types of interventions, for administrators to install certain collaboration schemes, and the district office to monitor school performance using an ultimately narrow set of criteria, it's ironic that you have more available to you as a teacher today than any other generation of teachers before. All you have do is reach out for what you need - and give what you know will do your students well, and everyone will be better for it.

Please don't misunderstand. We hear about all the pain during our live events and talks and visits to your schools. Educators are hurting everywhere right now. I, myself, received a significant paycut these past years as extra classes dried up and I had to take on multiple jobs to support my family. At the same time, if you step into any of the events in which we take part, or attend any outside professional development, you will definitely encounter educators walking on the edge of what's expected and bringing forth innovations and ideas rarely seen in traditional public school classrooms and rarely discussed in mandated trainings and interventions. Beneath our noses, while our professional development as teachers can often seem partially focused upon a segment of our work with students, a whole group of educators has taken it into their own hands to become the best human beings they can possibly be - all so they can become better, happier, and more of a blessing to those they serve. Do you feel this spark teeming inside of you? We hope you feel the desire to become a better human being, so you can assist your students in doing the same.

As this book comes to a close, we would like to offer you a part in the shifts that educators are taking, largely under the radar, throughout the Western World. It is our opinion that these shifts greatly hint at what the school can be for future generations - if only enough educators decide to pick up the mantle of the World's Greatest and proudly parade it upon their shoulders. Before you read about these shifts and decide if you are willing to take these up as an educator, we want to first honor you for what brought you here and what moved you to read through this book. Pause for a moment and consider this: What brought you to read this book? What are you being called toward as an educator? Can you see all the way to the horizon, or can you see only the first step in front of you? We encourage you to take that first step. As the education world marches onward down a path at which many educators roll their eyes, some World's Greatest Educators are walking in an entirely different direction. We invite you to keep your job, and take up the following shifts as well.

Shift #1: From content provider to curator.

For thousands of years, students came to educators to obtain knowledge. During this time, content was delivered solely by word-of-mouth and expensive texts. In the past two decades, the Internet has enabled any student to access any piece of content, anywhere, anytime, usually free of charge. Access to information is only going to increase over the next generation. The role, then, of the teacher cannot solely revolve around that of "content provider." We concede that while students largely rely upon their teachers to provide this content, this role will become more and more irrelevant as time moves forward. Educators must expand and deepen an aspect of their profession that up until recently they had largely ignored: Curating, or organizing, content into an impressive whole.

With all the media that students can conveniently access, educators must take up the role of being far more impressive and persuasive in their delivery. They have to provide a value that is not offered outside their classroom. If you think about the best teachers that you have ever had, you probably don't think, "Wow, I loved that teacher because they had the best worksheets EVER." Instead, you were probably moved by their way of being in the classroom, the way they interacted with the content, and the value that they delivered to you as a unique human being.

To become the curator of your classroom space, you'll have to advance yourself as an educator in some key areas. First, you'll have to become a better human being - better at teaching; better at handling stress; better at being rested, refreshed, and energetic. Second, you'll have to be willing to advance your training beyond that which you already have. You have been trained how to be a content provider; the kind of person who organizes information into amazing learning experiences; you will need an entirely different skillset. Finally, you'll have to reach beyond the confines of your classroom to gain support from allies beyond your walls. Your students can access the best educators in the world on video, so embrace the best and bring it (or them) into your classroom.

Shift #2: From expecting more to inspiring more.

With all the focus upon testing, accountability, and all students making it across the "finish line," we sometimes forget two things. First, we forget that we created the finish line and can move it anywhere we want. We define who wins and who loses. Second, we forget that each student has a different finish line and uses different capacities to get there than another student. Imagine walking into a gym and seeing a big sign on the wall which reads, "Quota: three push-ups." Accordingly, you get down on your hands and knees and do just those three pushups. Immediately, the owner of the gym walks up to you and says, "Gee! What proficiency! We have your workout room over here"; you are then ushered to a room full of workout equipment specially designed for your fellow, three-push-up people. "But I want to go over there!" you say, pointing to another room designed for the ten-push-up crowd. The owner turns to you with a grin and says, "Don't worry, son, you'll be retested next year and might be able to move over there in about eighteen months!" You would not tolerate this for your thirty-minute workout, but this is exactly what we do to students in many cases. Notice that our students often take our queues from what is expected from them. When the expectations are high and we afford them inspirational support to rise, they will often surprise us. It's not about setting high expectations so students do more; it's about providing the support needed for them to be more, and giving them plenty of opportunities to show us their growth.

Educators who have gotten the bug of "focusing upon developing the individual capacities of each student," spend most of their time developing and inspiring each student rather than waiting for the year or the next year to run its course. To get under the skin of your students to inspire them to do better, you have two options. First, you can be the kind of person they admire and want to follow. Second, you can be the kind of person that represents ideals with which they identify, even if they don't like you as an individual person. You can make the shift to become a better human being and inspire greater action in your students.

Shift #3: From being trained to being embodied.

I entered my coaching training because I wanted to be able to better impact the students with whom I worked. One of the things I felt I was really good at was listening. After some time in my coaching training, one of my Mentors said to me, "Guy, you act like your capacity to listen is like a list of steps – if you just do it a certain way, you'll get it right. You need to learn how to be a listener in your bones – like it's your nature, not some activity that you are taking up for the day." For nearly two years, I was assigned the task of meditating once per day for at least ten minutes. In meditation, you are not zoning out; instead, you are remaining completely aware of yourself and your surroundings. It was through this training that I was able to start listening to people without the mental clutter that I was constantly bringing to the table. I began to notice myself truly hearing people more fully, rather than my own ideas of what I thought I had heard. Over this journey, I was able to begin (and I stress "begin") the journey toward embodying the qualities that I am seeking as a listener.

Similarly, this movement from the trained, mechanical, step-by-step to the embodied-in-my-skin approach is one being taken up by educators who are on the edge of this education revolution that we have discussed herein. Paradoxically, this shift seems to ask the least of us (become more intimate with our training to such a degree that it's second nature) as we already have the training. However, this shift, actually, calls for the greatest versions of ourselves imaginable. To embody the qualities that you wish to bring to your school, you have to be willing to work for years in developing the capacities needed and tearing down the walls that stand in opposition. To start down this path, one needs to find a Mentor, coach, or spiritual friend who can work with you to name those qualities you want to develop and assist you as you resist the change required.

Shift #4: From cant's to cans.

No learner is like another. No teacher is like another. Every person on your campus is completely unique as a being. In the past decades, educators have made amazing strides to recognize the exceptionalities of each student. However, we have clearly seen an emphasis placed upon the exceptional difficulties experienced by learners - rather than the exceptional gifts they bring into the classroom. While it is entirely appropriate to know and leverage the knowledge we hold about our students' limitations and needs, it is our opinion that not enough is being done to draw the attention of educators to where it is needed most: to recognizing the gifts, talents, and skills that are represented in each of our students. Rather than spending so much time focusing solely upon the "cant's," we can include the "cans" as well. Consider: What gifts do your students possess? How could you utilize those in your classroom to benefit the learning you are facilitating therein?

Further, so much good could be made possible, simply by recognizing the gifts, talents, and skills of all educators that *already* sit within your building. With so many districts, schools, and programs clamoring for more money to do more outside staff development, they often ignore that the answers are often just down the hall. Chances are, there are amazing educators within your midst that have the answer you are seeking. When reaching outside your school for training, don't forget to recognize the new "cans" that these highly trained educators received at that conference, workshop, or event. Today, there are people at your school that are waiting for you to call upon them. Will you give them the gift of honoring their expertise? Will you allow them to serve your school? They may be waiting for you to call upon their talents.

Shift #5: From how to why.

Much of what is being discussed in education today is about "what we teach" (content knowledge) and "how we teach" (pedagogy). When Park was in his first years of teaching, he fell into the most common trap that all educators step into during these fragile opening moments: He began to focus exclusively upon these questions of the what and how. The problem that Park, and most others who are in their first years teaching, experienced is that they *really* don't know the precise answers to these questions. Accordingly, like many others, Park began acting like something he was not. Have you ever experienced the difference between how an educator interacts with his or her class of students when they are alone versus when the principal is in the room? Some teachers have mastered the art of symmetry, where the "me" in one's class full of students is the same as the "me" when an administrator is observing. To truly become our best selves as educators, we have to step outside much of the conversation about educators today and step outside of our expectations of "who we should be" and "what we should be doing" to ask a very simple question: "Why?"

Why do you teach? Think about that question for a second and feel it in your bones. Why do you teach? Have you ever experienced that moment as a teacher when what is happening between you and the students is in *perfect* sync with why you are teaching? When you uncover your "why" for teaching, everything changes. When difficulty arises, as it is bound to during your work, you are strengthened by the immense power of the "why." It is the intention that fuels you and fuels your work with your students. When your "why" holds the powerful intention to change lives and impact the futures of all students, working with the most difficult students only becomes part of living out your mission. When your "why" is willing to work immensely hard with one student, just to see their life exponentially influenced, you are willing to do this for almost anyone. When you start with figuring out your "why," and bringing that into the forefront of your work each day, you are truly on the road to becoming the "World's Greatest Me."

Remembering Kiley, Alyssa, and Austin

Do you remember Park's granddaughters that we mentioned at the start of this text? For me, being a young guy with no kids, at the time, I had never had someone as close to me as my Mentor, Park, go through such a life-altering predicament. For me, this stirred up major questions and insecurities about my own safety, those of my students, and those of my future children. The glaring questions that began seeping into every part of my teaching was, "Am I pulling the plug on this kid? Am I only teaching the Austins? How far am I willing to go to change this student's life and impact their future?" The morning that we were at that event with hundreds of students and Park took to the stage, knowing the whole time that his granddaughters were fighting for their lives down the road at the hospital, I could picture the skilled, attending physicians being their World's Greatest - just to live out the "why" of their calling. At the most basic level, in the weeks and months ahead, I was

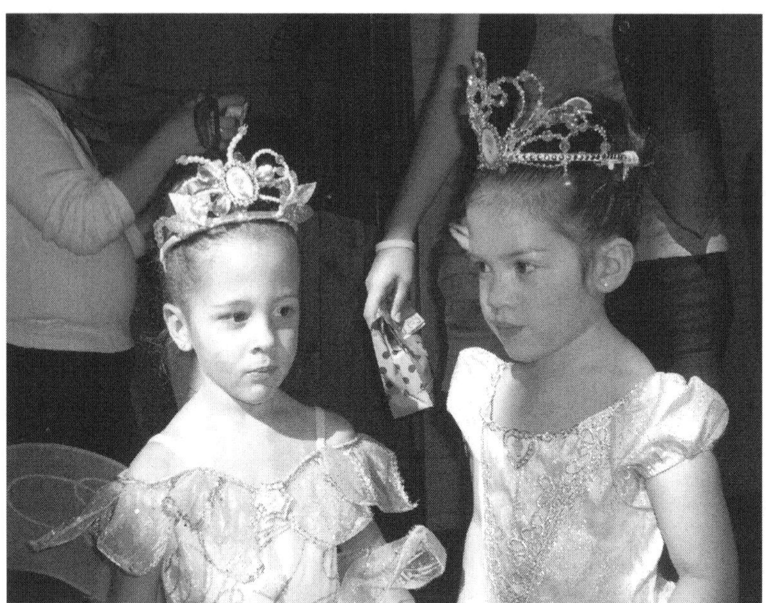

inspired to take up a way of teaching that was life-saving, future-altering, and soul-inspired. What would it mean for me to teach as if this kid's life depended on it?

We feel immensely honored to bring you this book. I have had the benefit of my Mentor, Park, who has been carrying the World's Greatest High School™ Philosophy for years before we even met. You now have the benefit of hearing about something that revolutionized our ways of teaching and working with our students, peers, parents, and community. Our greatest hope is that you are able to take that which you have read here and bring the World's Greatest Values to your school. As Park's Kiley and Alyssa are now entering elementary school, and now that Austin, his über-strong grandson, is following close-behind, I know that Park thinks each day about the type of schools that are waiting for them in their academic futures. For me, I now have a daughter of my own who will be stepping onto her first campus in just a few years. What kind of world in school's do I want to create for her? In your own heart, think about the kind of schools that you want to bring to your students, as if they were your own flesh-and-blood children.

We Honor You

The students of this world need you more than ever as their teacher. With all the chaos that is happening around the globe - and right down the street - the world is waiting for teachers like you, who have taken up the World's Greatest Values, to step fully into your highest calling as an educator. The question that truly needs to be answered as you read these closing words is "Will you answer their call to become the World's Greatest Me? In these moments, when many of the loudest educators are asking the wrong questions, will you have the fortitude and bravery to ask the right questions? Will you have the courage to point to the broader and deeper values that underpin what we do each moment of our day as educators? Today is the day to take up that calling.

Take up the calling to become the World's Greatest Me so you can do the work that our students need. Go out today and *Build the World's Greatest High School*. Now is the time to start. Each morning it starts anew as you walk onto campus; see students passing in the hallways; notice your peers setting up their classrooms for the day; and walk into that empty, dark room which you will soon fill with all that you have to offer. Why are you teaching today? Everyday is a great day to change lives and impact futures. Create the kind of school where the banner above the front gate could read, "Through These Doors Pass the World's Greatest." Thank you for who you are.

- Park and Guy

Afterword

Richard Parkhouse

Building the "World's Greatest" Philosophy is like selecting a restaurant for a memorable moment. Think about the selection process you go through for a special restaurant that will help you to celebrate a very special occasion. If you are planning to take your significant other out to celebrate an anniversary, you don't usually visit a fast-food type establishment to create that memorable moment. You look for the right location, the right attitude of the staff, and a rich ambiance inside the building. The type of building may be old and historic or it may be brand new and high-tech. You know you are someplace special when you first walk in the door and look around. The treatment by staff and their attitude contributes greatly to the experience and feeling of importance that is being communicated right from the beginning. The actions of others really matter and affect your attitude. You can tell you are in a quality establishment from the moment you walk in the door. The World's Greatest High School creates the same feeling. The building could be historic or very modern, and it's not about the ideal location or building, it is not the walls: it's what goes on within the location and walls. Just like that very special restaurant, you know you are in a special place when you first step inside, that first contact with the staff within, and what is being communicated by their brand provides a feeling of being in a "World's Greatest" school.

The World's Greatest High School™ Philosophy started to develop in my early years as an educator. I wasn't aware that I was formulating the concepts at first. The experiences, situations, staff, and the students I encountered helped me to understand my "Why" in building the World's Greatest High School. Looking back on my first year of teaching made me realize that the experiences, interactions and the contacts I had come across were the defining moments for me. I didn't understand the importance of those experiences on the development of creating a school wide culture and climate of inclusion for all stakeholders until thirteen years later.

The What

My journey as an educator began at 10:30 on a Sunday night in February of 1977. I was hired as a new teacher for the second semester due to increased enrollment at the school. I was in my classroom the night before preparing for my first day. The excitement I was experiencing was just like the anticipation I felt on Christmas Eve anticipating Christmas morning. I was truly looking forward to meeting my first-ever group of students. This was my first opportunity to, "Change Lives and Impact Futures!" I was working late to prepare my classroom to insure everything was perfect and in place for my "Grand Opening." There was a surprise knock on the door. I cautiously walked over to the door and peeked out. To my surprise, there was a sheriff with his gun pulled asking me, "What are you doing?" I was shaking trying to explain that I was a new teacher preparing for my first day. He asked for my school identification. "Oh no," I told him, I had not received any type of district I.D and tomorrow was going to be my very first day. I guess I was able to convince him that I was a new teacher as I was able to find a school document with my name on it: at least he did not arrest me.

Looking back on that moment and the significance of the sheriff's question, "What are you doing?" truly was one of the seeds to *Building the World's Greatest High School*. When I look back today, the sheriff's question, "What are you doing?" led me to reflect that I didn't know what I was doing. I was excited about working with my new class of students, but was not sure my students were excited about working with me. When they walked in and saw a new teacher, they had big smiles on their faces. It was not a happy smile, but the devious smile that suggested they were ready to test me and take me for a ride. After a couple of months of struggling and experiencing frustration in the classroom, I became aware of how my students were selected. Each teacher was asked to select three students that would be moved from their class to form a new class for our new teacher, Mr. Parkhouse. Well, low and behold, guess who was in my class? I can just imagine the thought process that every teacher went through as they contemplated which students would be transferred out. I'm sure they were thinking, "What would my class be like if these three students weren't in my class?" So my first experience as a teacher was with a group of outcasts and non-performers and I focused on working with who they were and adjusted my approach to reach each of them.

The Who

My view of teaching changed tremendously from the excitement and passion I had for, "Changing Lives and Impacting Futures" to questioning my decision to become an educator. I had lost sight of why I decided to become an educator. The thought continually crossed my mind as to 'Why" am I doing this and maybe I didn't have what it takes to be an educator. The "Why" was not clear to me at the time, but it played a key part in the years to come and I didn't really understand how significant that experience was at the time. I was so frustrated and the feeling of incompetence at not being able to reach these students was overwhelming. The major problem was in the "How" was I teaching and not my understanding "Who" I was teaching.

In education, mentors are a necessity, and I had formed a tremendous friendship with Mr. Jim Green, a master teacher at inspiring and challenging students, and who brought the best out of people. I have never seen anyone work magic with kids as Jim did. I will never forget the conversations we had that changed "Who" I was and "What" I was doing. Jim, told me, "I've watched you coaching on the baseball field and I've seen you in the classroom. You are a different person on the field and in the classroom, you need to bring your attitude, style, and methodology you use as a coach to inspire, stretch and challenge your players on the field into the classroom. You need to remember that a classroom teacher and a coach are both doing the same thing: teaching!" It was at that moment that I realized my insecurities as a teacher were causing me to fail miserably. I was trying to live up to what I thought a teacher should be and how a teacher should act. It created a conflict within and I was not being myself. I wasn't comfortable being "me" and this was a noteworthy point in my career. I had to become me: so I became "Park" and stopped trying to be someone that I was not. It was the beginning of the process where I started to employ my unique gifts, talents, and skills as to who I was as a teacher. I always wanted to be like Jim Green, and I finally realized that I couldn't be Jim but I could take what Jim offered and make it Park. This was the point where I started to take a realistic look at my strengths and weaknesses and the development of the "World's Greatest

Me." It was the moment where I became comfortable with who I was and I truly began my journey as an effective educator!

The last day of my first year of teaching, the principal came to my room. He walked over to me and told me he knew I had a difficult year, but he hired me because he saw something special in me. I will never forget him putting his arm around my shoulder and saying, "I know it was a challenging year for you, but because of this experience there will never be a class you can't handle!" It was the day of confirmation and a gratifying moment as an educator.

Over the next ten years I continued to evolve the "How" and the "What" of effective teaching and the development of "Who" I was and "Who" I was teaching. The early years were instrumental in the formation of the World's Greatest High School™ Philosophy. It began with the sheriff asking, "**What** are you doing?" It was the "**How**" am I going to deliver an effective lesson, it was the clarification of "**Who**" I was as an educator and the understanding of "**Who**" I was teaching. The strength came in the understanding and clarification of the most important question: "Why."

The Why

Looking back on these events, I see the importance in insightfully understanding the "Why" we do what we do at school. The "Why" is the power behind the creation of the World's Greatest High School. We must always challenge ourselves to question "Why" we are doing what we do. If we address the "WHY" we can build the World's Greatest High School, and then the "What," the "Who," and the "How" will fall into place.

Building the World's Greatest High School was written for the purpose of assisting educators in building a school culture that focuses on high, attainable expectations that stretches greatness from within all students and staff. The World's Greatest High School respects and supports everyone's unique talents. It is a place that acknowledges accomplishments of these individual gifts and talents and creates an environment built upon self-worth. It is a place that allows individuals to explore several avenues for future success. The World's Greatest High School™ Philosophy is about the importance of FUTURES for all students and building an environment that challenges everyone to be better today than yesterday.

The World's Greatest High School is a school where the everyday life is built upon relationship development within each person, their peers, their teachers, and everyone that their path may cross. One's success in life can be attributed to the relationships we have with others. When you think about success in life, it comes from others who gave us the opportunity to utilize our own gifts. They saw something special in us and gave us the opportunity to succeed. The relationship development process must occur from the first moment one has contact with the school until the moment they walk across the stage at graduation and beyond. The relationship between the teaching and learning process and the school environment is essential to the creation of this cultural and philosophical foundation for the school. What opportunities are you giving students, staff, and parents to be successful and perform at the World's Greatest level? The question is to what level are we challenging ourselves to achieve: there is "No Hope" in what I do; it's okay to be "Mediocre Me;" or the World's Greatest Me.

The power of what you communicate through your school brand and messaging will set the tone for expectations and the relationship they will have with the teaching and learning process. All of this holds true from the moment staff, parents, and community members walk on campus. What do you see when you enter the school? What is showcased in the front office? What messages are being communicated as you walk the hallways? What is the attitude, feeling, and engagement being demonstrated through each persons actions? It's just like when you walk into that special restaurant to celebrate that special occasion. Are you planning to go to a fast food restaurant or a classy establishment?

Hopefully, you had the opportunity to explore and challenge your thoughts of building a stronger school climate and culture. Dr. Guy and I wanted this work to stimulate, motivate, and challenge the "Why" you do what you do. Our intent is to provide challenges at the end of each chapter as a means to identify your current situation and apply thoughts, philosophies, methodology, and inspiration to start the process of making your school the World's Greatest! This is not an arrogant attitude where there is only one World's Greatest High School. The one where you go to school or teach can become the World's Greatest because of YOU! Every school should be working to become the World's Greatest. We have a very important task at hand: kids' futures are at stake! We must remember that every day is an opportunity to "Change Lives and Impact Futures" and this happens daily at the World's Greatest High School.

So, start with the "Why" being the driving force behind building the World's Greatest High School then start creating the best experience for your school family. Ask the "Whys" for building this for the Kileys and the Alyssas, the Austins, and all students. The "Whats" and "Hows" will fall right into place.

We must never stop chasing the WHY! Go out and become your "World's Greatest!"

- Park

Glossary

Academic Rally: A campus-wide celebration where the gifts, talents, and skills of all are intentionally put on display. Staffulty, students, parents, alumni, and community business partners are honored for their roles in helping others become the World's Greatest Me. Inspirational stories of the growth and the role of Mentors in these stories are tangibly illustrated.

Expectations: The anticipated futures that we hold for ourselves, our peers, and our students.

Mediocre High School: A loosely held-together school community that is "okay being okay." People at this school are not challenging themselves or each other to be better than the day before, or their way about challenging one another is inconsistent or ineffective.

Mentors: Those persons who advocate and assist another person in becoming his or her World's Greatest Me.

No Hope High School: A fractured school community that feels that kids don't care, which in-turn translates to the kids feeling that their school doesn't care, creating a place where largely no-one cares. People at this school say,

"You don't understand our kids," "you don't know their challenges," and "they can't learn."

Plans, Planning: the steps that we set to fulfill the expectations that we hold for ourselves, our students, our peers, our school, etc.

Relationships: the means by which the value system of the school is transmitted from one person to another.

Royal Family: The typically recognized sub-set of students, community members, staffulty, at any school. These include, but are not limited to popular athletic teams such as football and basketball or the players therein; straight-A, perfect attendance, and honor roll students; and Homecoming and Prom Kings and Queens. All schools have a Royal Family that is made up of people who are nearly always celebrated and/or put on the display as success at your school. The Royal Family represents a minority of the school population, such as the academic or athletic top-ten percent.

World's Greatest High School: a school community that has collectively agreed to take up and live out the World's Greatest Values.

World's Greatest Me: a person who is intentionally, consistently developing themselves to become better than the person they were the day before.

World's Greatest Values: the six core beliefs of the World's Greatest High School community.

About the Authors

Richard Parkhouse

"Everyday is an opportunity to Change Lives and Impact Futures."

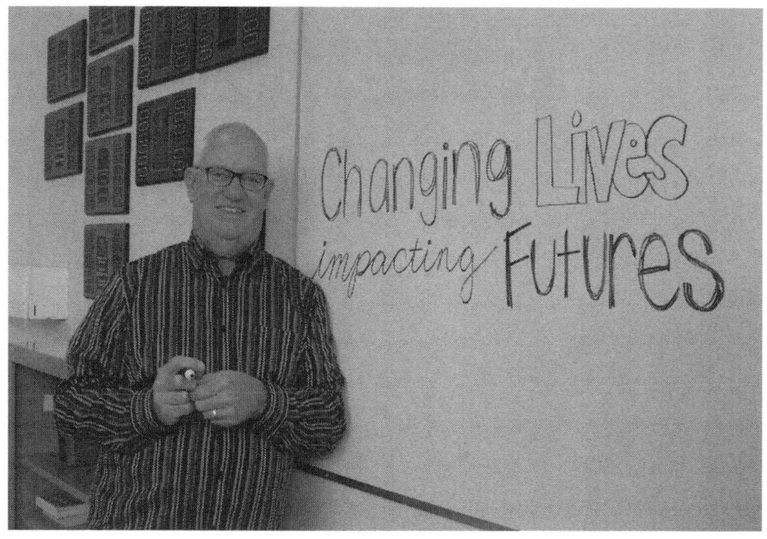

Known throughout educational circles as "Park," he brings a wealth of knowledge regarding the transformation of school cultures and increasing school-wide expectations. Park has dedicated himself to developing outstanding student activity and leadership programs nationally. He has been the keynote speaker at the CADA State Convention. He has also spoken at CADA Student Leadership Conferences, ACSA conferences, Jostens® Renaissance® National

Conferences, and at the National Association of Student Councils Conference. Park is an active member of the California Association of Activities Directors (CADA) and has written articles for the NASSP Student Leadership Magazine. Park's efforts have received national recognition as an Earl Reum Award Recipient, which recognizes those who mentor the trainers of student leaders. He is a member of the CADA Hall of Fame and was selected for his ability to instill a vision of schoolwide excellence for all. As a National Presenter for Jostens® Renaissance®, Park was inducted into the National Jostens® Renaissance® Hall of Fame in the first inaugural class in 1998. This honor was due to his commitment to helping develop Jostens® Renaissance® schools nationally, as well as being the founder of the Academic Pep Rally. He has served as an educator for twenty-five years as a science teacher, coach, Activities Director, and assistant principal.

During the past eleven years, Park has been working with over 1000 schools as an educator consultant with Jostens, Inc. His forte is the development of positive and interactive school climates. His work includes the development and implementation of bringing the core values of the schools alive, connectedness of student and staff, increasing the role of student leaders on campus, addressing the recognition gap on campus, and focusing on incorporating the core value of teaching and learning into the daily rituals of the school culture. Park's vision is to assist schools in taking their mission statement from artwork on the wall to where you can see it and feel it as you walk the halls. He is a master of creating environments where acknowledgement and recognition is deserved, specific, and meaningful for all stakeholders.

Park presents a wide variety of strategies that have proven to have a lasting effect on schools. These initiatives will bring information and knowledge, but more importantly, staff and students will be involved in the process of enhancing the school climate and effectiveness. The key to the success of his techniques is to create ownership for the stakeholders of the school. This in turn will help to keep the vision and philosophies at the forefront for years to come.

Jostens® and Renaissance® are registered trademarks of Jostens, Inc. and used herein with permission.

About the Authors

Guy E. White, Ed.D.

www.exitingthebakesale.com

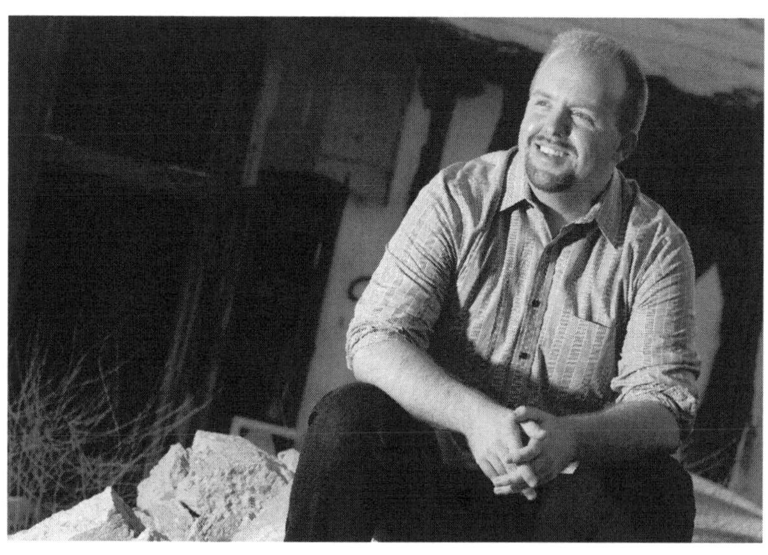

Dr. Guy E. White is the founder of Exiting the Bakesale®, the revolutionary fundraising system for schools wanting to raise money without selling wrapping paper and cookie dough. Guy's books, videos, products, online trainings, coaching and appearances inspire those he serves throughout the world. For these works, those he serves recognize him as providing life shifting, in-depth development programs for educators.

Guy holds the highest level of teacher certification available in the United States. He is a Certified Integral Coach™ by Integral Coaching Canada. Guy has "gold standard" accreditations in the teaching and coaching fields respectively.

Guy has contributed to Leadership in Student Activities magazine published by the National Association of Secondary School Principals for members of the National Association of Student Councils, the National Honor Society, and the National Junior Honor Society. His research, carried in multiple online research databases, on Activities Directors of highly successful secondary schools is one of the most recent and comprehensive bodies of research on high school co-curricular activities programs in the world.

Meet him and receive more free training at **www.exitingthebakesale.com**

Integral Coach™ is a registered trademark in Canada owned by Integral Coaching Canada Inc. and licensed to Guy E. White.

www.worldsgreatesthighschool.com

Made in the USA
San Bernardino, CA
29 August 2013